A PERFECT 10
– Party Edition!

Full Menus and Activities to
Make Hosting Parties a Breeze

TIM MULLIGAN

Copyright © 2023 by Tim Mulligan

All rights reserved. Published in the United States of America. No part of this book may be reproduced or transmitted in any form or by any means, graphic, electronic or mechanical, including photocopying, recording, taping or by any information storage or retrieval system, without permission in writing from the publisher.

This edition published by Highpoint Life Books
For information, write to info@highpointpubs.com.
First Edition

ISBN: 979-8-9879203-6-7

Library of Congress Cataloging-in-Publication Data
Mulligan, Tim
A Perfect 10 Party Edition
Full Menus and Activities to Make Hosting Parties a Breeze

Summary: "Following on the success of Tim Mulligan's *A Perfect 10* cookbook, this all-new follow-up features ten proven, go-to recipes for seven different types of parties, including weekend brunch, happy hour, birthday party, pool party, baby/engagement shower, Awards Shows/Superbowl, and the holidays. Party menus include ten delectable dishes for each event, plus cocktails/mocktails, glassware, fun games, activities, general ice-breaking craziness and other party essentials."
—Provided by publisher.

ISBN: 979-8-9879203-6-7 (paperback)
1. Cooking 2. Entertaining

Library of Congress Control Number: 2023914690

Cover and Interior Design by Sarah M. Clarehart
Photo Credits: All food photos taken by Tim Mulligan.
Cover and back jacket photos by Teresa McCann.

Manufactured in the United States of America

Dedication

To all the home cooks and party throwers out there—a strong and mighty army. I'd like to thank all who helped with this book, and came to the parties to eat, be merry, and provide feedback—this includes family (Cadey/Sean/Grace/Jon/Kelli/Taylor/Paul/Corey/DaNae), my inner circle (Binghams/Youngs/Doggetts/Doreen/Lori), and friends from far and wide (MP/Dan and family/Richlanders/Kevin/Ed/Ron/Christopher/Michael/Ken). Party on...

Table of Contents

Introduction ix
The Best Weekend Brunch 1

1. Drinks—Fizzy Fun Pink Lemonade and Partridges in Pear Trees.................................3
2. Appy—Ooey Gooey Hot Curry Cambozola Dip 5
3. Appy—Rosemary Spiced Candied Bacon 7
4. Side—Blueberry Almond Butter Smoothies...........................9
5. Side—Breakfast-y Pasta Salad 11
6. Main—Cheesy Egg and Polenta Casserole 13
7. Main—Fluffy Green Onion Cloud Eggs 15
8. Main—Chorizo Hash 17
9. Dessert—Chocolaty Goodness Coffee Cake.......................19
10. Dessert—Princess Leia Cinnamon Roll Apple Pie 21

Helluva Happy Hour..23

1. Drinks—Vodka Giddyups and Beer-Perol Surprises 25
2. Appy—Cocktail Meatballs with Grape Jelly..........................27
3. Appy—Mini Sausage Corn Pups...29
4. Appy—Baked Bacon Crackers 31
5. Appy—Zestylicious Mexi Layered Dip....................................32

6	Main—Mac and Cheese Station	35
7	Main—Loco Moco Nachos	36
8	Main—Mini-Chicken and Waffles	39
9	Dessert—Irish Cream Delectable Chocolate Brownies	41
10	Dessert—Honey-Butter Shortbread Cookies	43

Boffo Birthday Party 45

1	Drinks—Mulligan Micheladas and Lemon Chiffon Punch	47
2	Appy—Cubano Tots!	49
3	Appy—Party Popovers	51
4	Salad—Almondy Caesar Salad	53
5	Side—Yummus! Yogurt Dip	55
6	Main—Lemony Fettucine Alfredo	57
7	Main—Spicy Veggie Lasagna	58
8	Main—Blackened Flank Steak and Corny Salsa	61
9	Dessert—Pineapple Bacon Upside-Down Cake	63
10	Dessert—The BEST Birthday Cake with No-Churn Ice Cream	65

Perfect Pool Party 67

1	Drinks—Orange Shandys and Hemingway Daiquiris	69
2	Appy—Pimento Dip	71
3	Salad—Watermelon-Mint Salad	73
4	Salad—Antipasto Salad	75

5	Salad—Hawaiian Macaroni Salad	77
6	Side—BBQ Beans with Turkey Bacon	79
7	Main—Grilled Chicken Cobb Salad	81
8	Main—Grilled Turkey-Apple Burgers	83
9	Dessert—Chocolate Cold Brew Pistachio Cake Cups	85
10	Dessert—Pretzel Salad Cups	87

Not Your Average Shower! 89

1	Drinks—Sublime Sangria (Boozy and Not Boozy)	91
2	Appy—Cheesy Olive Puffs	93
3	Salad—Delectable Curry Chicken Salad	95
4	Side—Your New Favorite Coconut-Cilantro Rice	97
5	Side—Cup o' Grapes Fruit Salad	99
6	Main—Pickle-Craving Finger Sandwiches	101
7	Main—Tasty Turkey Picadillo Cups	103
8	Main—Tiny Thai Basil Beef Bowls	105
9	Dessert—Lovely and Lemony Olive Oil Cake	107
10	Dessert—Lemon-Lime Chiffon Pie, Oh My!	109

Awards Show Party! 111

1	Drinks—Pimm's Cups and Strawberry Bubblies	113
2	Appy—The Quick(est) and Easy(iest) Amazing Layered Dip	115
3	Appy—Greek Pita Walking Taco Snack Bags	117

4	Side—Alluring Arugula Pear Salad	119
5	Main—Mouthwatering Chicken Mole Tostadas	121
6	Main—Can't-Eat-Just-One Western Sliders	122
7	Main—Tantalizing Texas-Style Bean Soup	125
8	Main—Primo Parmesan-Crusted Chicken Strips	127
9	Dessert—Hazelnutty Goodness Carrot Cupcakes	129
10	Dessert—Mandarin Cream Delights	131

The Perfect Festive Holiday Dinner 133

1	Drinks—Tom and Jerrys and Spicy Holiday Lemonade	134
2	Appy—French Onion Soup Stuffed Mushrooms	137
3	Appy—Kale Mashed Potatoes	138
4	Side—Fried Brussels with Appley-Fenneley Slaw	141
5	Side—Spicy Creamy Cheesy Corn	143
6	Main—Tim's Turkey Milanese with Arugula Salad	144
7	Main—Perfect Pork Loin with Chunky Applesauce	146
8	Dessert—Dreamy Lemon Ginger Cake	149
9	Dessert—Blueberry Oatmeal Crisp with No-Churn Ice Cream	150
10	Dessert—Aunt Pat's Chocolate Espresso Cream "Pie"	153

Index 155

INTRODUCTION

Here it is...a follow-up! In 2022, I published my first cookbook, *A Perfect 10: Ten Proven, Scrumptious Recipes for Each Part of Every Meal*, where I shared a collection of favorite recipes I've curated over the years for seven different meal periods. Those seventy recipes represented decades of home cooking for friends, families, and colleagues — and I was pleasantly surprised by the great reception that book garnered.

So...I'm back! With another book of seven different Top 10 lists — this time focused on PARTIES! I love planning parties. I thrive on setting a theme, making a menu, cooking it all up for friends and family, and bringing people together for a great time.

In this book, I focus on seven types of parties — from a weekend brunch to a happy hour to a more fancy holiday dinner. For each, I've included a list of ten recipes, including drinks. I also provide recommendations on how you can "choose-your-own-adventure" for each menu — make it a small affair or go to town for a larger group and make all the recipes. You decide which route to go.

As a bonus, for each party I've included ideas for some fun games, activities, and general ice-breaking craziness.

These are more recipes from my own collection that I've saved, shared, created, repurposed, and collected over the years. From this home chef/amateur party planner-host to you: Have fun with it!

Tim Mulligan

THE BEST WEEKEND BRUNCH

Let's do brunch! Why, you ask? I could list a million reasons, but let's face it: You won't find a lot of things more fun than a great boozy brunch. There are a few basic rules to make a brunch truly special. For one, it needs to be leisurely — don't rush it! It's a great opportunity to relax, socialize, SLEEP IN, and chill with friends and family. Foodwise it gets tricky — you want breakfast items and lunch items, hence the word, right? You need, of course, a few breakfast staples, but throw in some light lunch items as well. Fun, bubbly drinks will be expected. From the menu that follows in this chapter, I'd say pick and choose wisely – or make it all! I threw the party pictured here by making every one of the dishes — I did the desserts the night before, and the rest wasn't too difficult to whip up the morning of. Pop the cork and get the fun flowing!

PARTY GAMES

Of all my parties in this book, brunch games probably are less important. Brunches should be chill and relaxing as you simply enjoy each other's company and the great food and day drinks. One thing I always do for my parties is make a special music playlist. I create a few different playlists each year and use them for different parties. They are always a mix of old and new, and party attendees nearly always want the playlist, so I then share the list with them through the music app or program. However, if you really want a game, trivia games are always popular, and you could tie the questions to your playlist — name that tune, the year of the song, who the singer is, and so on. For prizes, it's always good to give away some extra bottles of bubbly!

Drinks—Fizzy Fun Pink Lemonade and Partridges in Pear Trees

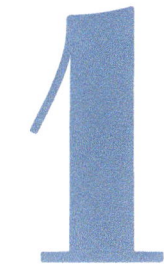

Your brunch guests will be expecting something fizzy and refreshing to drink. Here I offer two recipes for sparkling wine-based drinks. You can make either one, and also serve with, say, a Bloody Mary station — or do as I do and make a pitcher/carafe of each. Either way, these drinks definitely one-up the standard mimosa offering. They are refreshing, effervescent, celebratory, and F'ING DELICIOUS.

Fizzy Fun Pink Lemonade (6 glasses/1 pitcher)

- ☐ 1 750-ml. bottle sparkling rosé, chilled
- ☐ 2 ½ c. pink lemonade, chilled
- ☐ ¾ c. gin
- ☐ Mint leaves for garnish

1. In a large pitcher, stir together the sparkling rosé, lemonade, and gin.
2. To serve, set the pitcher next to an ice bucket (don't add ice to the pitcher) and place glasses around the pitcher. Garnish each glass with a mint leaf. Guests can help themselves by adding ice to a glass and pouring in the lemonade.

Partridges in Pear Trees (4 drinks/1 carafe)

- ☐ 1 c. pear juice (either store-bought or drained from canned pears)
- ☐ 4 rosemary sprigs
- ☐ 16 dried cherries or cranberries
- ☐ 1 750-ml. bottle prosecco
- ☐ Rosemary sprigs and pear slices, for garnish

1. In a large mason jar, combine the pear juice, rosemary sprigs, and cherries. Shake well.
2. Strain into a small pitcher or large carafe. Add the prosecco.
3. To serve, place flutes on the side of the pitcher. Garnish each glass with a spring of rosemary and a few pear slices. Serve up.

Appy—Ooey Gooey Hot Curry Cambozola Dip

Back in the day I waited tables at an Italian restaurant that served focaccia bread with a slab of creamy, nutty, Cambozola cheese on the side. I've been hooked since then. This dip is always a surefire hit — cubed Cambozola melts down beautifully, and topped with this curry-infused pecan mix, it's divine. Serve with whatever crackers and fruit you want — I think apple slices are the perfect vessel for it.

- ½ c. chopped pecans
- ½ c. dried cranberries
- 2 t. brown sugar
- ½ t. curry powder
- ½ t. kosher salt
- 1 lb. cubed Cambozola cheese (no rind)
- Crackers and apple slices, for dipping

1. Preheat the oven to 400 degrees.

2. In a small mixing bowl, combine the pecans, dried cranberries, brown sugar, curry powder, and salt. Mix well, then set aside.

3. Scatter the cheese cubes in a 9 x 9-inch (or close to it) baking dish. Sprinkle the pecan mix over the top, covering completely.

4. Bake for about 13 minutes, or until the cheese is melted and the nuts are toasted golden brown.

5. Serve with the sliced apples and crackers.

Appy—Rosemary Spiced Candied Bacon

Whatever recipes you choose from this Perfect 10 list, don't skimp on the bacon — it's brunch! People want their bacon! But instead of putting out a plate of greasy old bacon, I say fancy it up a bit: bake it with a peppery rosemary spread and serve it standing up in a mason jar — or on a platter — your call. Baking the bacon in this manner is everything, really — it's the easiest, most mess-free, and crispiest way to go. Yummy!

- ☐ 12 slices bacon
- ☐ 2 t. chopped rosemary
- ☐ 1 t. black pepper
- ☐ 4 T. sugar

1. Preheat the oven to 375 degrees.
2. Line a baking sheet with aluminum foil and set a wire cooling rack on top.
3. Lay the bacon slices on the rack. Bake for about 14 minutes, or until slightly crispy.
4. In a small bowl, mix the rosemary and black pepper. Set aside.
5. While the bacon is in the oven, combine the sugar and 2 teaspoons of water in a small glass bowl. Heat in the microwave for 45 seconds. Set aside.
6. Remove bacon from the oven. Flip them over. Brush the flipped side with the sugar water, then sprinkle with the rosemary pepper.
7. Return the bacon to the oven, and bake until browned all over, about 12 more minutes. Drain on paper towels.
8. Serve standing up in a mason jar or on a platter.

Side—Blueberry Almond Butter Smoothies

Who doesn't love a smoothie? Little smoothie shooters are a pleasant, refreshing addition to the brunch menu and provide a lighter alternative for those not wanting to go wild. I love them, and there's really no science around how to make them. I have played over the years with various combos of water, fruit, yogurts, protein powders — you name it. But for a no-fail brunch option, I like these little shooters of blueberry and almond butter. They're always a winner.

- ☐ 2 c. frozen or fresh blueberries
- ☐ 1 c. plain low-fat yogurt
- ☐ ½ c. low-fat milk
- ☐ 2 T. almond butter
- ☐ 2 T. maple syrup

1. Place all ingredients into a blender and blend until creamy and smooth. If it is too thick, add either a bit of milk or water to loosen it up.
2. Serve in small drinking glasses on your buffet. Smoothie shooters are a fun addition to the brunch table.

Side—Breakfast-y Pasta Salad

The thing to keep in mind about brunch menus is that it's not just breakfast food — it's a combination of breakfast and lunch (duh). So it's good to have a mix of the two. A fresh and vibrant pasta salad makes a beautiful (and unexpected) addition to your brunch table — and you can make it the night before! I like this breakfast-adjacent combination that ties in eggs and bacon. It's fresh and oh-so-tasty. The dressing is subtle and lemony. You can add more herbs if you want, but I don't think it needs it. Just don't skimp on the chive garnish!

- ☐ 8 oz. fusilli pasta
- ☐ 4 hard-boiled eggs, chopped
- ☐ 1 c. frozen peas
- ☐ 1 c. diced cucumbers
- ☐ ½ c. chopped cooked bacon (about 6 slices)
- ☐ ¼ c. mayonnaise
- ☐ ¼ c. sour cream
- ☐ 1 T. lemon juice
- ☐ ½ t. garlic, minced
- ☐ ¾ c. Parmesan cheese
- ☐ Kosher salt and black pepper, to taste
- ☐ Chopped chives, for garnish

1. Bring a pot of salted water to boil. Cook the pasta as the label directs. Drain and let cool.
2. In a large bowl, add the pasta, chopped eggs, peas, diced cucumbers, and bacon. Stir until combined.
3. In a small mixing bowl, combine the mayonnaise, sour cream, lemon juice, garlic, and Parmesan cheese. Add a pinch of salt and a few grinds of fresh black pepper.
4. Pour the dressing over the pasta mix and toss well.
5. Let chill before serving, up to a few hours.
6. Serve in a large bowl garnished with the chopped chives, or pre-fill small cups with a serving of the salad, each topped with the chives.

Main—Cheesy Egg and Polenta Casserole

This is one of those unique brunch entrees that not only tastes amazing, but is also a stunner on the brunch buffet. EVERY ONE of your guests will be asking for this recipe. Making a creamy, herby polenta is super easy — and polenta is the perfect vessel for a savory Italian board (make a big smear and throw yummy items on top), or use in this manner, with some sausage and eggs baked right into the polenta. It's so great and unique.

- ☐ 1 c. quick-cooking polenta
- ☐ 1 t. kosher salt
- ☐ 1 c. milk
- ☐ 2 T. butter
- ☐ 3 T. chopped thyme
- ☐ ½ c. shredded mozzarella cheese
- ☐ 8 oz. Italian breakfast sausage, sliced or cut into small chunks
- ☐ 1 c. torn spinach leaves
- ☐ 8 eggs
- ☐ ½ c. grated (or shredded) Parmesan cheese
- ☐ Black pepper
- ☐ ¼ c. shredded basil leaves

1. Preheat the oven to 400 degrees. Grease a 9 x 13-inch baking dish.
2. In a large saucepan, bring 4 cups of water to a boil. Once boiling, whisk in the polenta and salt, whisking constantly until the polenta bubbles up and pulls away from the pan, about 3 minutes.
3. Stir in the milk, butter, thyme, and mozzarella cheese until smooth and creamy.
4. Spread the cheesy polenta into the baking dish. Layer with the sausage and then the spinach. Make indentations for the eggs, and carefully crack each egg into each indentation. Sprinkle the Parmesan cheese over the top.
5. Bake for about 15 minutes, or until the egg whites are cooked and the yolks are soft-cooked.
6. Let it stand for a few minutes, then serve with a sprinkling of fresh black pepper and basil leaves on top.

Main—Fluffy Green Onion Cloud Eggs

There are a million ways to make eggs for breakfast or brunch, but none as visually striking as the light and fluffy Cloud Eggs! You can embellish these in a myriad of ways. Before baking the egg white "cloud," you can add whatever herbs, protein, and/or spice, you wish. I like to keep my clouds simple — I opt for green onion slices and then top them off with some Maldon sea salt flakes and pepper. These look beautiful on the brunch table!

- [ ] 6 large eggs
- [ ] 2 finely sliced green onions
- [ ] Maldon sea salt flakes
- [ ] Black pepper

1. Preheat the oven to 400 degrees. Line a baking sheet with parchment paper and coat well with cooking spray.

2. Arrange 6 little bowls and 1 large mixing bowl. Crack each egg and carefully slide the yolks into their own little bowl. Combine the whites in the large mixing bowl.

3. With an electric mixer, whip the egg whites until stiff peaks form. Use a large spoon to scoop 6 "clouds" of egg whites onto the baking sheet. Carefully sprinkle the green onion slices onto each cloud. Bake for exactly 4 minutes, when they should start to slightly brown.

4. Remove the clouds from the oven and use the back of a spoon to push a small indentation into the middle of each one. Carefully slide a yolk into each cloud. Return the clouds to the oven and bake for another 4 minutes.

5. Using a spatula, carefully remove each cloud and place them onto a serving platter. Sprinkle sea salt flakes and pepper on top and you are ready to serve!

Main—Chorizo Hash

This hash is super easy, and I can vouch that it is impossible to not nail perfectly. And the flavor! Buttery potatoes, zesty and spicy chorizo sausage, cooked onions and herbs — it's awesome. Serve it with the Cloud Eggs (see Recipe 7), or you can always add some poached or scrambled eggs to the mix. Make a lot — these are great as leftovers! I double the recipe every time, just to have a few bowls to nosh on during the week.

- [ ] 1 T. olive oil
- [ ] 1 white onion, diced
- [ ] 1 T. finely chopped fresh thyme
- [ ] 1 t. kosher salt
- [ ] ½ t. black pepper
- [ ] 8 oz. chorizo sausage
- [ ] 2 large Yukon Gold potatoes, peeled and cut into 1-inch cubes
- [ ] Hot sauce

1. Warm the oil in a large skillet over medium heat.
2. Add the onion, half of the thyme, salt, and pepper, and cook for about 10 minutes, stirring frequently, or until the onion is golden brown and soft.
3. Remove the casings from the chorizo, crumble, and then add to the onion pan. Cook for a couple of minutes, stirring well.
4. Stir in the potato cubes and the other half of the thyme. Cook for about 15 minutes, stirring occasionally. Add a few dashes of hot sauce and cook for another 10 minutes, or until the potatoes are softened and the chorizo is cooked. (I cover it during this last stint to ensure the potatoes cook well.)
5. Serve alongside the Cloud Eggs (see Recipe 7) or with poached or scrambled eggs on top.

Dessert—Chocolaty Goodness Coffee Cake

Coffee cake is so easy to make – nothing elaborate, accessible to all levels of home cook, and a quick fix when you need a brunch or breakfast addition to your party table. This recipe is one I've made since I was a kid — I just usually wing it on the filling. Today, I invited chocolate to the party, which was a very popular brunch party guest. It makes for a huge brunch hit.

Filling
- ☐ ¾ c. flour
- ☐ ⅔ c. brown sugar
- ☐ 1 t. cinnamon
- ☐ ½ t. kosher salt
- ☐ ½ c. chopped pecans
- ☐ 5 T. unsalted butter, softened

Cake
- ☐ 2 c. flour
- ☐ 1 t. baking powder
- ☐ ½ t. baking soda
- ☐ ½ t. kosher salt
- ☐ 8 T. (1 stick) unsalted butter
- ☐ 1 c. sugar
- ☐ 2 eggs
- ☐ 2 t. vanilla
- ☐ 1 c. sour cream
- ☐ 3 milk chocolate bars (1.55 oz.), broken into pieces

1. Preheat the oven to 350 degrees. Line an 8 x 8-inch baking dish with foil, allowing for an overhang.
2. Make the topping: In a small mixing bowl, combine the flour, brown sugar, cinnamon, salt, and pecans. Mix in the butter with your hands, using your fingers to squish everything together well. Set aside.
3. Make the batter: In a large bowl, whisk together the flour, baking powder, baking soda, and salt. In a standing mixer, beat the butter and sugar until light and fluffy. Add the eggs, beating well. Beat in the vanilla and sour cream. Once well mixed, add the flour mixture in batches until well mixed and the batter is thick and creamy.
4. Spread half of the batter into the baking dish. Spread the chocolate pieces on top. Spoon the remaining batter over the chocolate layer. Sprinkle the nut topping over the top.
5. Bake until the topping is golden brown and the cake is not jiggly in the middle, about 55 minutes.
6. Let cool complely. Use the foil overhang to pull the cake out of the pan. I like to cut it into small pieces and set the pieces out on a cake stand on the buffet.

Dessert—Princess Leia Cinnamon Roll Apple Pie

Because this is a brunch, I suggest offering a dessert that's a departure from your typical coffee cake. Why not serve this strange mash-up of good old-fashioned apple pie with cinnamon rolls baked right on top?! And who doesn't love to take a cinnamon roll slice and squish it to make Leia's infamous cinnamon bun hairdo? Have fun with it! It's so good.

- ☐ 2 sheets of store-bought pie crust
- ☐ 2 T. unsalted butter, softened
- ☐ ½ c. sugar
- ☐ 1½ t. cinnamon
- ☐ 5 peeled and sliced apples (Pink Lady, Granny Smith — your choice)
- ☐ Fresh juice of 1 lemon
- ☐ 1 t. vanilla
- ☐ 1 egg, slightly beaten
- ☐ ⅔ c. powdered sugar
- ☐ 2 T. milk

1. Preheat the oven to 400 degrees. Place one pie crust sheet in a 9-inch pie plate.

2. Lay the second pie crust sheet on a lightly floured surface. Spread the butter on top.

3. In a small mixing bowl, combine ¼ cup of sugar and 1 teaspoon of cinnamon. Sprinkle over the buttered pie dough. Roll the dough into a tight log. Cut the log crosswise into ½-inch slices. Set aside.

4. In a large mixing bowl, toss the apple slices with the lemon juice, vanilla, and remaining ¼ cup of sugar and ½ teaspoon of cinnamon. Spread the apples over the pie crust in the pie plate.

5. Take each cinnamon roll slice and, using the bottom of a drinking glass dipped in sugar, carefully flatten to about half the height. Spread each flattened cinnamon roll over the top of the apples. Brush the tops of the cinnamon rolls with the beaten egg.

6. Bake the pie on a baking sheet for about 50 minutes, or until the crust is golden brown and the filling is bubbling hot. Transfer to a rack to cool slightly.

7. For the glaze, whisk the powdered sugar and milk in a small bowl until smooth. Drizzle over the slightly cooled pie.

HELLUVA HAPPY HOUR

Who doesn't love happy hour? The traditional after-work happy hour is a good opportunity to get discounted food and drinks, try new places, and blow off some workplace steam. But for happy hours at your place, it's a different story — it's all about special cocktails, socializing, and generally catching up with friends and colleagues in a relaxed environment.

Key to your menu is good drinks. That is a must. And happy hour food can't be too heavy, since there still might be a dinner afterward. But others might see this as their meal for the night. I say it's best to plan either way — just serve some good drinks, some lighter appys, and some more substantial ones as well (you know I love a self-serve station). End with some finger food-style dessert options. This menu is a winner.

PARTY GAMES

For a happy hour, cue up your iPad or TV with an instructional line dance video and surprise everyone with an impromptu line dancing lesson. And don't get me started on drinking games — I love them — and a happy hour is the perfect time for this. My favorites include the following:

- Thumper — A drinking game where you must remember everyone's hand signals. Get the rules online! It's fun!
- Roxanne — Play the song *Roxanne* by The Police and make everyone drink every time Sting says "Roxanne."
- The ever-popular Fuzzy Duck — Take turns whispering "fuzzy duck" in the ear of the person to your right. When someone stops and says, "Jump back, duck," you switch directions and whisper "ducky fuzz" in the ear of the person to your left. Continue this stupid practice, reversing when one says, "Jump back, duck," and whenever someone mucks up the words, that person drinks (or is out, and you then continue until there's a winner).

Drinks—Vodka Giddyups and Beer-Perol Surprises

When people go to happy hour at a drinking establishment, normally it's all about nabbing a bargain price on a beer or stiff drink. But for a happy hour party at your place, turn this notion on its head and offer a great, unique cocktail that your guests will be surprised and thrilled by. These two drinks, I think, make for the prefect combo at a happy hour party. Vodka Giddyups, with its lovely cinnamon-clove syrup (make this in advance) added to vodka, is great for your spirits afficionados. For the beer drinkers, surprise them with a beer cocktail, something I personally love. Serve both and make this the happiest of hours for your guests. Each recipe makes 1 cocktail, but I like to make pitcher of them, by quadrupling Step 3, enough for 4 cocktails!

Vodka Giddyups

- ☐ 5 c. sugar
- ☐ 3 lemons, halved
- ☐ 18 whole cloves
- ☐ 4 cinnamon sticks
- ☐ 1 vanilla bean
- ☐ 1 c. lemon juice (fresh is best!)
- ☐ 1.5 oz. vodka
- ☐ Mint sprigs, for garnish

1. Make the cinnamon clove syrup: In a large pot, combine the sugar, 4 cups water, lemons, cloves, cinnamon sticks, and the vanilla bean, and stir well. Bring to a boil and then simmer on low heat for about 1 hour. Strain into a container and set aside.

2. Before serving, make the lemonade: In a mixing bowl or large mason jar, combine 1 cup of the cinnamon clove syrup, the lemon juice, and 1 ½ cups water, and shake or stir well. For a pitcher, I'd double this.

3. Make the cocktails: For each drink, add 1.5 ounces vodka and 4 ounces lemonade to a rocks glass. Add ice, give a stir, and garnish with a mint sprig. Or, quadruple that and make pitcher of them, pre-mixed.

Beer-Perol Surprises

- ☐ ¼ c. honey
- ☐ 3 oz. Aperol
- ☐ 2 oz. grapefruit juice
- ☐ 2 oz. fresh lemon juice
- ☐ Grapefruit bitters
- ☐ Pilsner beer
- ☐ Grapefruit twist, for garnish

1. Make the honey syrup: In small saucepan over medium heat, mix the honey with ¼ cup water and stir until the honey dissolves. Let cool.

2. In a pitcher, combine the Aperol, grapefruit juice, lemon juice, 2 ounces of the honey syrup, 8 dashes of the grapefruit bitters and stir well.

3. Serve on ice. Top each glass with a float of the pilsner and the grapefruit twist.

Appy—Cocktail Meatballs with Grape Jelly

My Aunt Pat, whose recipes I feature heavily in *A Perfect 10*, has been a cooking inspiration to me my whole life. While mostly known for her incredible baked goods, every holiday I would look forward to her homemade cocktail meatballs served in a spicy and tangy grape jelly sauce. I've seen variations of this recipe over the years, modernizing it, zipping it up — but not today. This is just Aunt Pat's incredibly easy (and unique — water chestnuts?) recipe, no Tim enhancements added. The combo of the sweet grape jelly and tangy chili sauce creates such a yummy and unique flavor, both sweet and spicy. Serve warm, even in a slow cooker or chafing dish if you have one, with cocktail toothpicks so your guests can dig right in.

- ☐ 2 lbs. ground beef
- ☐ 8 saltine crackers, crushed
- ☐ 1 small onion, diced
- ☐ 2 eggs
- ☐ 1 8-oz. can water chestnuts, chopped
- ☐ ½ t. kosher salt
- ☐ ½ t. black pepper
- ☐ 2 c. chili sauce
- ☐ 2 c. grape jelly

1. Preheat the oven to 350 degrees.
2. Make the meatballs: In a large mixing bowl, combine the ground beef, crackers, onion, eggs, water chestnuts, salt, and pepper. Mix together and then use your hands to roll approximately 4 dozen golf ball–sized meatballs.
3. Place the meatballs on a foil-lined baking sheet and bake for about 30 minutes, or until the meatballs are cooked through.
4. Make the sauce: Combine the chili sauce and grape jelly in a saucepan and heat over medium heat. Turn to low and let simmer for about 15 minutes.
5. Fold the meatballs into the sauce, ensuring full sauce coverage.
6. Serve in a chafing dish or a slow cooker, with a side of toothpicks.

Appy—Mini Sausage Corn Pups

This is the quintessential happy hour food item. Little finger foods that pack a punch. Who doesn't like an elevated mini corn dog (pup)? You can use any cooked sausage (chorizo, spicy, flavored — go nuts). And they are super cute, cooked in these mini-muffin tins. You can go with a store-bought dipping sauce like a grainy mustard, but believe me when I say my dipping sauce below is truly amazing — I've dubbed it TIMmustard sauce — and will become your go-to dipping sauce for, like, everything. Feel free to double this entire recipe. Your guests will be popping them like crazy.

- ☐ 3 fully cooked Italian sausages (your choice of flavor — I like spicy hot)
- ☐ 1 egg
- ☐ ¾ c. buttermilk
- ☐ ½ c. yellow cornmeal
- ☐ ¼ c. flour
- ☐ 2 t. sugar
- ☐ ½ t. kosher salt
- ☐ ½ t. baking powder
- ☐ ½ t. baking soda
- ☐ ¼ t. cayenne pepper
- ☐ 3 green onions, sliced
- ☐ ¼ c. Dijon mustard
- ☐ 2 T. honey
- ☐ 1 t. hot sauce
- ☐ 2 t. red wine vinegar

1. Preheat the oven to 375 degrees. Coat a 24-cup mini-muffin tin with cooking spray. Set aside.
2. Slice the cooked sausage into 24 slices (8 slices per sausage) about ½-inch thick.
3. In a small mixing bowl, whisk together the egg and buttermilk.
4. In a large mixing bowl, combine the cornmeal, flour, sugar, salt, baking powder, baking soda, and cayenne pepper. Mix well. Stir in the egg-buttermilk mixture. Stir in the sliced green onions.
5. Pour the batter into the muffin pan, filling each halfway. Place a slice of sausage into each muffin tin. Bake until golden brown and cooked through, about 12 minutes.
6. Make the TIMustard dipping sauce: In a medium mixing bowl, whisk together the Dijon, honey, hot sauce, red wine vinegar, and a tablespoon of water. Set aside.
7. Let the corn pups cool slightly, then remove from the pan. Serve with the dipping sauce.

Appy—Baked Bacon Crackers

Bacon-centric offerings are always a hit at happy hour, and these crackers do not disappoint. The bacon pretty much melts right into the cracker, resulting in a delish little bacon-y bite of heaven. You can drop the brown sugar if you want, but I think the sweetness with the bacon and Parmesan makes a fantastic combination. Cook 'em low and slow. They'll get gobbled up immediately.

- ☐ 1 c. Parmesan cheese, grated
- ☐ 1 c. brown sugar
- ☐ 2 T. cayenne pepper
- ☐ 2 T. black pepper
- ☐ 1 package/sleeve of club-style crackers
- ☐ 1 lb. thinly sliced bacon, each piece cut in half

1. Preheat the oven to 250 degrees. Place a baking rack on top of a baking sheet.

2. In a small mixing bowl, combine the cheese, brown sugar, cayenne pepper, and black pepper. Mix well.

3. Lay out the crackers on the counter or on a cutting board. On top of each cracker, place about 1 teaspoon of the cheesy-sugar mixture and spread it evenly. Carefully wrap a piece of bacon around the cracker, completely covering it. Place each wrapped cracker on the backing rack.

4. Place the baking sheet in the oven, and bake for about 1 hour and 45 minutes, or until the bacon is crisp and molded right onto the cracker.

5. Serve either right out of the oven or shortly thereafter.

Appy—Zestylicious Mexi Layered Dip

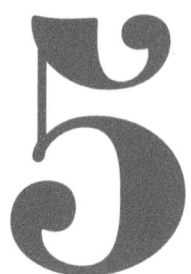

You may have noticed that this is not the only layered dip in this cookbook. I love a good layered dip, and most party guests do as well. For a happy hour, you need to have some sort of chip-and-dip situation, so you can't go wrong with this one. You can go store-bought for the beans, guac, salsa…but why, when they are so easy make and taste so much better? (Mulli Guacamole!) And this corn salsa is so good, you may want to double or triple the recipe to have on hand all week.

- ☐ 4 c. frozen corn, fire roasted if you can find it
- ☐ ¼ c. chopped cilantro
- ☐ 1 T. diced jalapeno
- ☐ Juice of 1 lime
- ☐ 1 small red onion, chopped (about 1 c.)
- ☐ 1 pint sour cream
- ☐ 1 t. coriander
- ☐ 1 t. smoked paprika
- ☐ Kosher salt
- ☐ Refried beans (see *A Perfect 10* cookbook, page 122)
- ☐ Guacamole (recipe at right)
- ☐ 5 oz. Cotija cheese, crumbled
- ☐ 3 radishes, thinly sliced
- ☐ 3 green onions, sliced
- ☐ Hot sauce
- ☐ Tortilla chips
- ☐ Lime wedges, for garnish

1. Make the fresh salsa: In a medium mixing bowl, toss together the corn (if you can't find fire roasted, then sauté the corn in a little olive oil, stirring, until the corn starts to brown/char), cilantro, jalapeno, lime juice, onion, and a pinch each of salt and pepper. Mix well.
2. Make the crema: In a small bowl, mix together the sour cream, coriander, smoked paprika, and 1 teaspoon of salt. Stir until smooth.
3. In a 9 x 13-inch or 10 x 10-inch baking dish, spread a thick layer of refried beans. Cover with a layer of guacamole.
4. Cover the guacamole with a full layer of the crema and sprinkle with the crumbled Cotija.
5. Spread the radishes and green onion over the crema. Drizzle a little hot sauce over the top.
6. Serve with tortilla chips and lime wedges.

Mulli Guacamole

- ☐ 3 ripe avocados, pitted
- ☐ ½ c. chopped cilantro
- ☐ ¼ c. chopped red onion
- ☐ Juice of 1 lime
- ☐ ½ c. Parmesan cheese
- ☐ 2 T. olive oil
- ☐ 1 t. kosher salt

Mix all ingredients, slightly smashing the avocados, to your desired consistency.

Main—Mac and Cheese Station

This might just turn out to be the most popular recipe at any of your parties. Ooey and gooey, full of flavor, easy to make — everyone loves this mac and cheese recipe. And it's perfect for a happy hour. Serve it warm along with a bunch of toppings that your guests can really go to town with. I promise you, it will be devoured. You can add any other toppings you desire — more cheese, different proteins, random chopped/sauteed veggies, sauces — it's a choose-your-own mac and cheese adventure.

- ☐ 1 lb. elbow macaroni
- ☐ 2 c. heavy cream
- ☐ 2 c. milk
- ☐ 3 cloves garlic, peeled and smashed
- ☐ 2 T. Dijon mustard
- ☐ 3 c. grated Gruyere cheese
- ☐ ½ c. grated Parmesan cheese
- ☐ ½ c. grated sharp cheddar cheese
- ☐ 1 T. Worcestershire sauce
- ☐ 1 T. hot sauce
- ☐ Salt and pepper
- ☐ Accompaniments: Sliced green onions, chopped Kalamata olives, chopped cooked bacon, toasted breadcrumbs, fried shallot slices

1. In a large pot, bring 10 cups of water to a boil. Add a generous pinch of salt. Add the macaroni, give a stir, and let cook for about 8 minutes. The noodles should be slightly al dente.

2. Drain the macaroni, reserving 1 cup of the pasta water.

3. In the same pot, combine the cream, milk, garlic, and reserved pasta water and bring to a low boil. Add the mustard and Gruyere and stir well. Add a pinch of the salt and pepper. Let cook, stirring, until the cheese melts. Add the Parmesan and cheddar, and stir until it's melted and the sauce is creamy and smooth. Add the Worcestershire and hot sauces. Stir well.

4. Add the macaroni and fold in to blend. Allow the macaroni to rest for a few minutes. If needed, remove the garlic cloves (they may have dissolved into the sauce by now).

5. Serve in a nice serving dish, a slow cooker turned on low, or a chafing dish. Set out little bowls for self-service.

6. For a mac and cheese bar, also put out some fun accompaniments: chopped cooked bacon, sliced green onions, fried sliced shallots, toasted breadcrumbs, chopped Kalamata olives, and even more Parmesan and hot sauce!

Main—Loco Moco Nachos

One of my family's favorite meals is the good old loco moco, which is a traditional Hawaiian dish – simply a bowl of white rice topped with a hamburger patty and covered with brown gravy and a fried egg. It's delicious. So for this menu, what's more popular for happy hour than nachos? Wham bam, mash the two up, and you have something unique, delish, and sure to get your guests talking and pigging out. Loco Moco Nachos. You're welcome.

- ☐ 1 ½ lbs. ground beef
- ☐ 2 T. teriyaki sauce
- ☐ 1 t. kosher salt
- ☐ 1 t. black pepper
- ☐ ½ onion, diced
- ☐ 1 c. sliced mushrooms
- ☐ 1 ½ c. beef broth
- ☐ 2 t. Worcestershire sauce
- ☐ 1 T. corn starch
- ☐ 10 flour tortillas
- ☐ 2 c. coconut-cilantro rice (page 97)
- ☐ 2 c. grated provolone cheese
- ☐ Hawaiian Slaw (recipe below)

1. Prepare the meat: In a large mixing bowl, combine the beef, teriyaki sauce, salt, and pepper. In a large skillet, cook the meat mixture over medium-high heat until browned. Set aside.

2. Make the gravy: Coat a medium saucepan with cooking spray and cook the onions over medium heat until they soften and start to brown. Add the mushrooms, and let cook a few minutes. Stir in the broth and Worcestershire sauce, whisking together until well mixed. Whisk in the corn starch and let simmer for about five minutes, stirring occasionally, until thickened. Use a blender to turn the mixture into a smooth brown gravy.

3. Make the chips: Cut each tortilla into 6 pieces. In a large skillet, heat 1 to 2 inches of coconut oil. When hot, fry the chips, flipping once, until golden brown. Let sit on a paper towel-lined plate.

4. Put it all together: In a large glass baking dish or cookie sheet, spread the chips along the bottom. Sprinkle a layer of rice over the chips, covered by a layer of meat, and a layer of cheese. Repeat with a second layer. Bake at 400 degrees until bubbling hot, about 15 to 20 minutes. Before serving, spoon the gravy over the top, and then sprinkle the slaw over the top of that.

Hawaiian Slaw

- ☐ 1 package coleslaw mix
- ☐ 1 15-oz. can crushed pineapple, drained
- ☐ 2 hard-boiled eggs, sliced
- ☐ ½ c. mayonnaise
- ☐ ¼ c. apple cider vinegar
- ☐ 2 T. brown sugar
- ☐ ½ c. chopped cilantro
- ☐ ½ t. salt
- ☐ ¼ t. black pepper

1. In a medium mixing bowl, mix the coleslaw with the pineapple and sliced eggs.

2. In a small bowl, whisk the mayonnaise, vinegar, brown sugar, cilantro, salt, and pepper together until smooth. Pour over the coleslaw mixture and toss to coat. Refrigerate until ready to serve.

Main—Mini-Chicken and Waffles

Chicken and waffles is really — let's just say it — f'ing awesome. So good for brunch, lunch, dinner, whatever. So why not make a cute handheld version for a happy hour? Also, included in this recipe is a great chicken nuggets recipe. (Yes, my first restaurant job was a McNugget fryer, hence my nickname McNugget Mulligan in high school). You can come back to this recipe often just for the yummy nuggets. But take those nuggets and put them on a mini waffle brushed with lemony butter and a drizzle of warmed maple syrup (and I like a bit of hot honey as well!), and you've got a happy hour winner.

- ☐ 1 lb. boneless chicken strips, cut into small sections (like a chicken nugget!)
- ☐ ½ c. sour cream
- ☐ ½ t. garlic powder
- ☐ ½ t. onion powder
- ☐ ½ t. smoked paprika
- ☐ Zest of 1 lemon
- ☐ Kosher salt
- ☐ Black pepper
- ☐ 5 c. corn flakes, crushed
- ☐ 2 T. olive oil
- ☐ 2 T. chopped fresh rosemary
- ☐ 24 frozen mini waffles (the smaller the size the better)
- ☐ 6 T. butter, softened
- ☐ Maple syrup

1. Preheat the oven to 450 degrees. Spray a rimmed baking sheet with cooking spray.
2. In a large bowl, mix the chicken pieces with the sour cream, garlic powder, onion powder, smoked paprika, half of the zest, and a pinch each of salt and pepper.
3. In a shallow dish, scatter the crushed corn flakes. Stir in the olive oil, half of the rosemary, and a pinch each of salt and pepper. Coat the chicken pieces in the corn flake mixture, tossing well to cover fully. Place each coated piece on the baking sheet and lightly spray with more cooking spray over the top. Bake until browned and cooked through, about 15 minutes.
4. Place the frozen mini waffles on another baking sheet, and bake for the same time as the chicken, but flipping halfway through. They should be cooked and slightly toasted and browned.
5. While those are cooking, combine the butter with the remaining zest and rosemary and a pinch each of salt and pepper.
6. After cooking, spread the lemon-rosemary butter on the waffles.
7. Place the waffles on a platter with a chicken nugget on top. Drizzle with warmed maple syrup and a drizzle of hot honey if you have some around!

Dessert—Irish Cream Delectable Chocolate Brownies

I mean...it is a happy hour. So why not have a boozy dessert? These fudgy chocolate brownies are good as is, but add a boozy cream cheese frosting — even better. Not just for the holidays anymore, the combo of unctuous chocolate and Irish cream is an awesome flavor combination. Since it's happy hour, I recommend cutting them into little squares.

Brownies
- ☐ 16 T. (2 sticks) butter
- ☐ 1 c. chocolate chips
- ☐ 1 c. brown sugar
- ☐ 1 c. sugar
- ☐ 4 eggs
- ☐ 1 t. vanilla
- ☐ ½ t. kosher salt
- ☐ 1 c. flour

Cake
- ☐ 4 oz. cream cheese, room temperature
- ☐ 8 T. (1 stick) butter, room temperature
- ☐ 2 T. Irish cream liqueur
- ☐ 2 c. powdered sugar
- ☐ Green food coloring

1. Preheat the oven to 350 degrees. Generously grease one 9 x 13-inch glass baking dish and line it with parchment paper with an overhang. Butter the paper as well.

2. For the brownies, bring a small saucepan of water to a simmer over medium heat. Place a glass bowl containing the butter and chocolate chips over the top. Let them melt, stirring often.

3. Using a stand mixer, combine the melted chocolate, brown sugar, sugar, eggs, vanilla, and salt, and mix well. Add the flour and mix until combined.

4. Pour the brownie mix into the prepared baking dish and bake for about 25 to 30 minutes, or until the center is not jiggly. Let them cool completely in the pan.

5. For the frosting, combine the cream cheese and butter in a medium mixing bowl, using electric beaters. Add the Irish cream liqueur and beat until well combined. Gradually mix in the powdered sugar and beat until nice and fluffy. If desired, take about 1 cup out of the mixture and add green food coloring to swirl the white and green together when frosting.

6. Spread the frosting over the cooled brownies, then let them sit in the fridge until the frosting is firm. Use the parchment overhang to remove the brownies from the baking dish. Slice into squares and serve!

Dessert—Honey-Butter Shortbread Cookies

These are really like the greatest cookies ever! You absolutely will not be able to stop eating them. It's something about the potato chips shortbread topped with a soy (!) glaze…with more potato chips on top. These were an internet sensation a few years back, and I've tweaked the many recipes out there to what I think is the perfect cookie. I like to keep them pretty small, and I cook them a bit soft. They are unique, cute, and utterly addictive.

Cookies
- ☐ 2 c. flour
- ☐ ⅔ c. sugar
- ☐ 1 t. salt
- ☐ 1 T. honey
- ☐ 1 c. crushed potato chips
- ☐ 1 c. salted butter

Glaze
- ☐ 6 T. butter, melted
- ☐ ¼ c. honey
- ☐ ¼ c. powdered sugar
- ☐ 1 t. salt
- ☐ 1½ t. soy sauce

1. Using a food processor, combine the flour, sugar, salt, honey, and crushed potato chips, pulsing repeatedly to form a dough.
2. Divide the dough in half. Use your hands to form each half into a log, rolling each log on the counter back and forth to elongate, then wrap each log in a long piece of plastic wrap. Let them chill in the refrigerator for at least 1 hour.
3. Preheat the oven to 350 degrees. Place parchment paper on a baking sheet.
4. After the dough is chilled, remove the plastic wrap and slice each log into ½-inch rounds, about 12 per log. Place the slices on the baking sheet, about 1 inch apart.
5. Bake for about 12 minutes, until the edges just start to brown. I like these a bit soft, and not crispy.
6. While cooling, make the glaze. Whisk the melted butter, honey, powdered sugar, salt, and soy sauce.
7. When cooled, dip the top side of each cookie into the glaze and let set up on a wire rack. Sprinkle the tops with some extra crushed potato chips.

BOFFO BIRTHDAY PARTY

I can't even begin to count the number of birthday parties I've planned, cooked for, and hosted over the years for my kids, family members, friends, coworkers, and sometimes even for strangers. Typically, on someone's birthday, you ask them what their favorite dish is, and serve that. Go for it. Or just use this tried-and-true menu and you're golden! For this menu, I include a bit of everything — three entrees (including a barbecued dish!), two vastly different types of birthday cakes, and an array of fun starters and salads. I hope it all works for you — and you really make someone's special day even more special!

PARTY GAMES

Birthday party games really depend on the age group, but let's say you are planning a party for teens or adults. One thing I often do is go online and make custom bingo cards using words specific to the birthday guest. Just use normal bingo rules, but use these words instead of the normal BINGO letters when calling. Give prizes for normal bingo, then move to a bat or a V, then go for the speed-round blackout. Always a crowd-pleaser.

Other party games I love to employ are Fibbage (available on a TV or computer), Farkle, Spoons (super fun with adults and adult beverages) — and never discount the old standby, charades. (Or for a rowdier crowd, try Running Charades — look it up!)

Drinks—Mulligan Micheladas and Lemon Chiffon Punch

For this birthday party, I'm making two very different drinks — Mulligan Micheladas and Lemon Chiffon Punch. There's something for everyone! I love a michelada so much — basically, it's beer with zesty spices (I skip the tomato/clamato juice, sorry). On the flip side, this beautiful and oh-so-simple punch will wow the guests and is beyond easy to make. Let the birthday shenanigans begin!

Pitcher o' Mulligan Micheladas
Makes 1 full punch bowl

- ☐ Fresh juice of 4 limes
- ☐ 1 t. Worcestershire sauce
- ☐ 8 t. hot sauce
- ☐ 4 12-oz bottles lager beer, chilled
- ☐ 1 t. kosher salt
- ☐ Lime wedges, for garnish
- ☐ Chili salt for rims of the glasses (optional)

1. Optional: On a plate, scatter the chili salt. In a small, shallow bowl, add the juice from one lime. Dip the rim of a serving glass in the lime juice and then in the chili salt. Set aside.

2. In a large pitcher, add the lime juice, Worcestershire sauce, hot sauce, beer, and salt. Mix well. Before serving, add ice cubes.

3. Serve in salt-rimmed (or not) glasses, over ice, with a lime wedge for garnish.

Lemon Chiffon Punch
Makes 1 pitcher / 4 full glasses

- ☐ 2 lemons, sliced
- ☐ 1 750-ml. bottle prosecco or Champagne
- ☐ ½ bottle white wine
- ☐ 1 pint lemon sherbet or sorbet

1. Make frozen lemons: Place the sliced lemons on a baking sheet in the freezer. Freeze for a few hours, or overnight.

2. In a large pitcher, add the prosecco and the wine. Mix well.

3. When ready to serve, add a few cups of ice to the pitcher, some of the frozen lemon slices, and with some small scoops of the sherbet.

4. Serve alongside small glasses, with the remaining frozen lemons as a garnish.

Appy—Cubano Tots!

Who doesn't love Tater Tots? They might be one of my favorite guilty pleasures of all time. I've got an arsenal of Tot recipes that I use (maybe a future cookbook?), but for this birthday celebration, to really elevate the Tot, this is the way to go — Cubano them up! You might want to double this recipe since they are so easy to just grab and pop into your mouth. I've yet to be at a party where they weren't the first dish to be wiped clean.

- ☐ 1 12-oz. bag frozen Tater Tots
- ☐ 4 t. yellow mustard
- ☐ 8 slices thin deli ham
- ☐ 1 large dill pickle, finely chopped
- ☐ 8 slices Swiss cheese

1. Place the Tater Tots on a baking sheet and cook per the package instructions.

2. Using a work surface or large cutting board, spread out the ham slices. Slather about ½ teaspoon of mustard on each slice. Sprinkle about 1 teaspoon of the diced pickle on top of the mustard. Top with a cheese slice.

3. Using a pizza cutter, slice the ham lengthwise into ¾-inch strips. Wrap a ham strip around a cooked Tater Tot and stick a toothpick through the middle to hold it together.

4. Preheat the oven to broil. Place the wrapped Tater Tots onto a baking sheet coated with cooking spray.

5. Broil for a few minutes, or until the ham begins to crisp up and the cheese is nice and melty.

6. Serve on a platter and wow your guests!

Appy—Party Popovers

I'm not big fan of throwing a basket of rolls or store-bought bread onto a table and calling it a day. So for this menu, which begs for a bread component, I'm adding these little beauties. This is a great recipe for your collection — you can switch out the cheeses, add different spices, shake it up however you want. What are popovers? They are light and fluffy — and hollow — baked pastries. They get their name due to the fact that they "pop over" the top of the baking pan while cooking, which results in a puffy, airy, hollow, and super-cute and fun party table addition. This recipe makes 12 popovers — you may want to double or adjust this recipe accordingly to make more of these beauties.

- ☐ 4 eggs
- ☐ 1 c. flour
- ☐ 1 t. kosher salt
- ☐ 1 t. fresh ground black pepper
- ☐ ½ c. heavy cream
- ☐ 1 c. milk
- ☐ 2 T. butter, melted
- ☐ ¼. c. fresh thyme, chopped
- ☐ 1 c. diced ham
- ☐ ½ c. Asiago cheese, grated

1. Preheat the oven to 400 degrees. Spray a 12-muffin tin with cooking spray.
2. In a large mixing bowl, combine the eggs, flour, salt, and pepper using an electric mixer until well mixed.
3. Slowly add the heavy cream, milk, and butter and mix well. Stir in the chopped thyme.
4. Sprinkle the diced ham on the bottoms of the muffin tins and then add the batter, filling each tin about ⅔ full. Sprinkle the Asiago on the top of each muffin tin.
5. Bake for 35 minutes, until puffed out and golden brown. These are best served warm.

Salad—Almondy Caesar Salad

You've heard me wax poetic on salads — how much I love them and also how important it is to surprise your guests with yummy, craveable variations. And this version of a Caesar — albeit totally nontraditional — is so good, and very almond-forward (a good thing!). You'll come back to this recipe for all types of parties in your future.

- ☐ 4 c. cubed dense bread (ciabatta, focaccia)
- ☐ ½ c. olive oil
- ☐ ½ c. sliced almonds
- ☐ ⅔ c. shredded Parmesan cheese
- ☐ Zest and juice of 1 lemon
- ☐ Kosher salt
- ☐ Fresh ground black pepper
- ☐ 2 t. Dijon mustard
- ☐ 1 garlic clove, minced
- ☐ 8 oz. red leaf lettuce
- ☐ ⅔ c. shaved Parmesan cheese

1. Make the croutons: Preheat the oven to 425 degrees. In a large mixing bowl, toss the bread cubes with ¼ cup of the olive oil, ¼ cup of the almonds, ⅓ cup of the shredded Parmesan, lemon zest, and a large pinch of salt and pepper. Spread on a baking sheet and bake for about 8 minutes, or until the croutons are slightly toasted.

2. Make the dressing: In a food processor or blender, combine the remaining ¼ cup of olive oil, remaining ¼ cup of sliced almonds, remaining ⅓ cup of shredded Parmesan, lemon juice, mustard, and garlic. Blend until smooth and then season with a pinch of salt and pepper.

3. In a large mixing bowl, toss the lettuce with the dressing and the croutons. Scatter shaved Parmesan cheese on the top.

4. Serve on a large platter.

Side—Yummus! Yogurt Dip

Making hummus at home is super fun and so easy. Just a few simple ingredients and a few minutes of your precious time yields a delicious and fresh hummus dip. For this recipe, I lightened it up with the addition of plain yogurt. It results in a lighter dip that is super flavorful. Serve this on your buffet table with nice chips, crackers, and vegetable crudité. Yummus!

- ☐ 1 garlic clove, minced
- ☐ 2 15-oz. cans garbanzo beans, drained and rinsed
- ☐ ½ cup plain yogurt
- ☐ 2 t. white wine vinegar
- ☐ 1 t. cumin
- ☐ ½ t. salt
- ☐ ½ t. black pepper
- ☐ Pomegranate seeds and dried basil, for garnish (optional)

1. Mix all ingredients except the optional garnishes in a blender until smooth.

2. Transfer to a serving bowl, drizzle with olive oil, and sprinkle a few pomegranate seeds and a smattering of dried basil on top if desired.

3. Serve with chips or vegetable crudité.

Main—Lemony Fettucine Alfredo

For this birthday party menu, I included three different entrée choices, and I say pick two of the three — either both pastas, or one or the other and the steak dish — your call. Having worked for many years in Italian restaurants, believe you me, I've served countless bowls full of just about everybody's favorite pasta, good ol' fettuccine alfredo. I love this version of the classic recipe, which I completely amplify with lemon and shallots. It will be the hit of any birthday party!

- ☐ 12 oz. fettucine noodles
- ☐ 1 ¼ c. heavy cream
- ☐ 1 egg yolk
- ☐ 2 t. lemon zest
- ☐ 1 T. butter
- ☐ 1 shallot, diced
- ☐ ⅓ c. Parmesan cheese
- ☐ Kosher salt
- ☐ Fresh ground black pepper

1. Cook the fettuccine per the package instructions. When done, drain, and reserve about 1 cup of the pasta water.
2. While the pasta is cooking, in a small mixing bowl, whisk together the heavy cream, egg yolk, and lemon zest. Set aside.
3. In a large saucepan, melt the butter and then add the diced shallot. Cook for a few minutes, or until lightly browned.
4. Reduce the heat to low and whisk in the cream mixture and the Parmesan. Whisk for a few minutes, or until slightly thickened. Season with about ½ teaspoon each of salt and pepper.
5. Toss the fettuccine with the sauce. If too thick, add the reserved pasta water to get to a nice saucy consistency.
6. Serve in a large bowl, topped with more Parmesan and a few turns of fresh ground black pepper.

Main—Spicy Veggie Lasagna

I've been making this particular lasagna, with varying substitutions of vegetables, for at least 30 years. It was a favorite of my mother's and graced our family table on many, many occasions, including family birthday parties. The constants here are the beautiful basil oil and puttanesca sauce. For the roasted veggies you can make any substitutions you want! Or just follow this recipe and enjoy.

Basil Oil

- ☐ 2 cloves garlic, minced
- ☐ 2 c. basil leaves
- ☐ 1 c. olive oil
- ☐ 1 t. kosher salt

Combine ingredients together in a blender. Set aside.

Puttanesca Sauce

- ☐ ¼ c. olive oil
- ☐ 1 c. onion, diced
- ☐ 5 cloves garlic, minced
- ☐ 2 28-oz. cans crushed plum tomatoes
- ☐ 1 c. Kalamata olives, chopped
- ☐ 2 T. tomato paste
- ☐ 2 T. capers, drained
- ☐ ½ t. dried basil
- ☐ ½ t. crushed red pepper flakes

Heat the olive oil in a large pot over medium heat. Add the onion and cook until lightly browned, about 5 minutes. Add the garlic and cook a few minutes more. Add the remaining ingredients and let simmer until slightly thickened, about 40 minutes. I like to use an immersion blender to make it a bit smoother, but that's your preference.

Roasted Vegetables

- ☐ 2 red bell peppers, cut into strips
- ☐ 1 large onion, cut into slices
- ☐ 2 c. mushrooms
- ☐ ¼ c. olive oil
- ☐ Kosher salt

Toss all ingredients together in a mixing bowl. Spread onto a baking sheet and broil for about 8 minutes, stirring occasionally. The veggies should be well cooked and starting to brown.

Put It All Together

- ☐ 2 lb. ricotta cheese
- ☐ 1 lb. no-boil lasagna noodles
- ☐ 2 c. mozzarella

1. Preheat the oven to 350 degrees. In a medium bowl, mix the ricotta cheese with ½ cup of the basil oil made previously, and 1 teaspoon salt.

2. Lightly grease a large baking dish. Spread about ½ cup of the puttanesca sauce in the bottom. Cover with a layer of lasagna noodles. Top the noodles with a layer of the ricotta mixture and then ½ of the roasted vegetables. Add a layer of shredded mozzarella cheese and then ½ of the sauce. Repeat another layer, and end up with mozzarella on top.

3. Bake for about 1 hour, or until browned and bubbly. Let it sit for a least 15 minutes. Drizzle the rest of the basil oil over the top before serving.

Main—Blackened Flank Steak and Corny Salsa

For a non-pasta option for this birthday party, I include a go-to entrée that I've made for parties for years now — it's a simple grilled flank steak with a tasty spiced-up rub and a delicious corn salsa to pour over the top. It's delicious. Serve with some of the salsa on the side along with some good tortilla chips.

Steak and Corn Salsa

- ☐ 1 2 lb. flank steak
- ☐ 3 c. corn kernels (you can grill 3 ears or use frozen, charred if possible)
- ☐ ¼ red onion, diced
- ☐ 1 jalapeno, seeded, diced
- ☐ 1 c. cherry tomatoes, halved
- ☐ 1 c. cilantro, finely chopped
- ☐ ½ c. fresh lime juice
- ☐ Kosher salt
- ☐ Fresh ground black pepper

Dry Rub

- ☐ 2 T. brown sugar
- ☐ 1 T. chili powder
- ☐ 1 T. paprika
- ☐ 2 t. kosher salt
- ☐ 2 t. fresh ground black pepper
- ☐ 1 t. cayenne pepper
- ☐ 1 t. garlic powder
- ☐ 1 t. ground mustard
- ☐ ½ t. coriander
- ☐ ½ t. cumin

1. Make the dry rub: In a small mixing bowl, combine all ingredients and mix well. Set aside.

2. Prepare the meat: Drizzle a few tablespoons of olive oil onto the steak and rub it in all over. Then coat the steak with the dry rub, covering it completely. Let the steak sit in the refrigerator with the rub for 1 to 3 hours.

3. Make the salsa: In a medium mixing bowl, combine the corn, onion, jalapeno, tomatoes, cilantro, and lime juice. Add a pinch of salt and pepper. Set aside. (You can also make this the night before.)

4. When ready, grill the steak, turning it occasionally, until it is nicely charred and medium rare, about 4 to 5 minutes per side. Transfer the steak to a cutting board and let it rest for about 10 minutes.

5. Slice the steak in thin strips and place nicely on a serving platter. Sprinkle the corn salsa over the top of the steak, and if any is left over, serve the remainder in a small bowl on the side along with tortilla chips.

Dessert—Pineapple Bacon Upside-Down Cake

For a birthday party I always like to make two desserts. For this party, I've chosen a traditional birthday cake and a nontraditional birthday cake as well. (It's always great to keep your guests surprised and guessing!). For the nontraditional option, your guests will be blown away by this modern take on the classic pineapple upside-down cake — modernized with, of course, bacon.

Brownies
- ☐ 6 slices bacon
- ☐ 12 T. (1 ½ sticks) butter, softened
- ☐ 1 c. brown sugar
- ☐ 7 pineapple rings
- ☐ 7 maraschino cherries
- ☐ 2 c. flour
- ☐ 1 ½ t. baking powder
- ☐ ½ t. baking soda
- ☐ ½ t. kosher salt
- ☐ ¾ c. sugar
- ☐ 2 eggs
- ☐ 1 t. vanilla
- ☐ ¾ c. buttermilk
- ☐ Maraschino cherries, for garnish

1. Preheat the oven to 350 degrees. Cook the bacon in a large skillet until crisp. Remove the bacon to a plate lined with a paper towel, and pat down to remove grease. Finely chop the bacon and set aside.

2. Keeping the bacon grease in the skillet, add 4 tablespoons of the butter and melt it over low heat. Once melted, pour the butter into a 9-inch round cake pan, ensuring it covers the bottom. Sprinkle the brown sugar evenly over the top.

3. Place the pineapple rings on top of the brown sugar, fitting in as many as you can. Sprinkle 3 tablespoons of the chopped bacon over the top, making sure you get in-between the slices and in the centers.

4. In a medium bowl, whisk together the flour, baking powder, baking soda, and salt.

5. In a large mixing bowl, beat together the remaining stick of butter with the sugar until light and fluffy, a few minutes. Beat in the eggs and vanilla.

6. Beating on low speed, slowly add the flour mixture to the wet mixture, followed by the buttermilk. Beat until you have a smooth cake batter. Fold in the remaining chopped bacon.

7. Spread the batter in the cake pan on top of the pineapple. Bake for about 1 hour, or until the top is nicely caramelized and the cake is set. Transfer the cake to a cooling rack, let cool for about 15 minutes, and then invert onto a platter. Decorate by adding a maraschino cherry to the center of each pineapple ring. Let cool before serving.

Dessert—The BEST Birthday Cake with No-Churn Ice Cream

Every birthday party needs a good old-fashioned, traditional birthday cake. And this simple chocolate cake with white chocolate frosting is a stunner. Sometimes simple and classic is the route to take. And my family has enjoyed this particular classic birthday cake for, like, decades. Enjoy this with my No-Churn Ice Cream (recipe on page 151) and consider stirring sprinkles or chocolate chips into the ice cream!

Cake
- ☐ 12 T. (1 ½ sticks) butter
- ☐ 1 c. milk
- ☐ ¾ c. unsweetened cocoa powder
- ☐ 1 ¾ c. sugar
- ☐ 2 ¼ c. flour
- ☐ ½ t. baking powder
- ☐ ½ t. baking soda
- ☐ ½ t. salt
- ☐ 3 eggs
- ☐ 1 t. vanilla

Frosting
- ☐ 8 oz. white chocolate, chopped
- ☐ 24 T. (3 sticks butter), softened
- ☐ ½ t. salt
- ☐ 2 ½ c. powdered sugar
- ☐ 1 ½ t. vanilla
- ☐ Any chocolate sprinkles or candies you want (I used sprinkles and malted milk balls for this one!)

1. Preheat the oven to 325 degrees. Generously grease two 8-inch round cake pans and dust with cocoa powder. Combine the butter, milk, and ½ cup water in a saucepan and bring to a low simmer. Transfer to a large bowl and stir in the cocoa powder and sugar, whisking until smooth. Let cool for about 5 minutes.

2. In a medium mixing bowl, whisk together the flour, baking powder, baking soda, and salt. Set aside.

3. Whisk the eggs and vanilla into the cocoa mixture. Once mixed, add the flour mixture in batches and stir until well combined.

4. Divide the cake batter between the two pans, and bake for about 35 minutes, or until the cake is set and not jiggly in the middle. Let the cakes cool for about 10 minutes and then invert them onto a rack to cool completely.

5. Make the frosting: Place the white chocolate in a glass bowl and microwave in 30-second intervals, stirring after each interval, until smooth. Let cool slightly. In a large mixing bowl, beat the butter and salt until fluffy, about 3 minutes. Beat in the melted white chocolate until well combined. Gradually add the powdered sugar and beat until smooth and fluffy. Stir in the vanilla.

6. Frost both layers, one on top of the other. Decorate with the chocolate candy or sprinkles.

PERFECT POOL PARTY

No one loves a pool party more than yours truly. I love pool party food, pool party drinks, pool party games, pool party music playlists — everything about them. Always have and always will. Living in Palm Springs now, I throw them regularly and try to wow my guests with a guaranteed day o' fun.

Key to a great pool party are each of these elements: food that's not too heavy and also leans into a picnic vibe (of course, use that BBQ if you have one!), drinks that you can load into big plastic glasses with ice and serve from pitchers or coolers, organized games with prizes that you can play in the pool, and a playlist that gets your guests groovin' in and around the water. I daresay this menu does the trick and will cause a SPLASH at your next backyard bash!

PARTY GAMES

For a pool party, definitely, you need an awesome playlist. Like I do with other parties, share the playlist with the guests after they leave.

During the party, I love to create a floating table in the pool with air mattresses (either single or stacked on top of each other), and play Farkle or other dice games. Other traditional pool games — like Marco Polo, chicken fights, water-noodle relay races — are always fun with a little booze thrown in the mix.

Drinks—Orange Shandys and Hemingway Daiquiris

While I'm personally not a big beer drinker, nothing shouts pool party to me more than a shandy. A what? A shandy is a fun summer drink, typically a mash-up of beer and some nonalcoholic beverage, like lemonade or a carbonated soda. It's a delicious and refreshing low-alcohol drink. I love them, and this is my go-to shandy recipe, which substitutes orange juice for lemonade. Complement that with a boozy pool party drink, and why not a daiquiri? A daiquiri is a classic cocktail typically comprised of rum, lime juice, and sugar. Simple and elegant, you can blend it up with crushed ice and serve it straight up or on the rocks. And this Hemingway version is so yummy — rumor has it that this was Ernest Hemingway's favorite drink — and it drops the sugar and adds grapefruit juice and maraschino liqueur. Let's get the party started!

Orange Shandys
Makes a pitcher, with 4 full drinks

- ☐ 6 c. wheat beer
- ☐ 1 c. orange juice
- ☐ ½ t. almond extract
- ☐ 1 orange, thinly sliced, for garnish

1. Combine the beer, orange juice, and almond extract in a large pitcher and mix well.
2. Serve on the rocks or straight up, with the oranges as a garnish.

Pitcher o' Hemingway Daiquiris
Makes a pitcher, with 4 full drinks

- ☐ 8 oz. white rum
- ☐ 2 oz. maraschino liqueur
- ☐ 3 oz. lime juice
- ☐ 2 oz. grapefruit juice
- ☐ Lime wheels for garnish

1. Add all ingredients to a large pitcher. Stir or shake vigorously to mix well.
2. Serve with ice and a lime wheel.

Note: You can also blend them with ice to make a frozen Hemingway Daiquiri.

Appy—Pimento Dip

You have to include a dip (or two) at your pool party, and this recipe is as good as it gets. What is pimento dip? Last year I was lucky enough to take a trip through the South, and it literally turned into a tour of pimento dip variations. We tried so many iterations of this beauty — some spicy, some savory, some sweet. The beauty of this dip is that you can shake it up however you see fit. The mainstay ingredients are typically mayo, shredded cheddar and other cheeses, and of course chopped pimentos (sweet and tangy little red peppers). My friends and family seem to love my version below — give it a spin!

- ☐ 4 oz. cream cheese, softened
- ☐ 8 oz. mild cheddar cheese, shredded
- ☐ 8 oz. pepper jack cheese, shredded
- ☐ 4 oz. jar diced pimentos
- ☐ ½ red onion, diced
- ☐ 1 c. mayonnaise
- ☐ 2 garlic cloves, minced
- ☐ 1 t. smoked paprika
- ☐ ½ t. salt
- ☐ ½ t. pepper
- ☐ Crackers, for serving

1. In a large mixing bowl, stir together all ingredients until well mixed.
2. Test for seasoning level. Add more salt and/or pepper if desired.
3. Place in the refrigerator until ready to serve

Salad—Watermelon-Mint Salad

Every party needs something lighter on the menu, particularly a pool party. And to me, a refreshing and vibrant watermelon-mint salad is the perfect addition to the festivities. Sweet watermelon perfectly meshes with aromatic mint. Throw in some fresh summer berries and fresh lemon zest, and you've got a winner. Serve in individual-sized cups or a large serving bowl. You can also throw a few of the sweet fruit pieces into your summer cocktail!

- ☐ ¼ c. sugar
- ☐ 4 mint leaves
- ☐ Zest and juice of 1 lemon
- ☐ Kosher salt
- ☐ 2 c. berries (blackberries, blueberries, or raspberries)
- ☐ 3 c. watermelon, cut into small cubes
- ☐ Mint leaves, chopped, for garnish

1. In a small saucepan, bring the sugar and ¼ cup of water to a boil. Remove from the heat, add the mint leaves, and let it sit for about 15 minutes, then remove the leaves.
2. In a large mixing bowl, toss together the berries, the watermelon, and the sugar-mint syrup.
3. Serve with chopped mint leaves sprinkled on the top.

Salad—Antipasto Salad

As I've espoused in my blogs and in my original *A Perfect 10* cookbook, nobody wants a boring old green salad. The challenge I bestow on you is to build up an arsenal of great, easy, unique salads, which are particularly important for an outdoor party like this one. This salad takes all the best parts of an antipasto plate — marinated veggies, salami, cheeses, and fruit, and turns it on its head into a mighty fierce salad. And it looks gorgeous on your buffet table. You can always use this as a base recipe and then throw in whatever antipasto "goodies" you like — make it a choose-your-own antipasto salad adventure!

- ☐ 2 T. Kalamata olive brine
- ☐ 1 t. Dijon mustard
- ☐ ½ c. olive oil
- ☐ 8 oz. spinach leaves
- ☐ 4 oz. arugula
- ☐ Some combination of:
  - o ½ c. Kalamata olives, chopped
  - o ½ c. marinated mushrooms, halved
  - o 8 oz. fresh mozzarella balls
  - o ½ c. glazed pecans or walnuts
  - o 4 oz. Parmesan cheese, shredded
  - o 1 jar (7 oz.) marinated artichoke hearts, quartered
  - o 8 oz. cherry or grape tomatoes, sliced
  - o 1 pear, thinly sliced
  - o 4 oz. salami, sliced
- ☐ Croutons or bread sticks
- ☐ Store-bought Balsamic glaze
- ☐ ½ c. fresh basil leaves, torn

1. Make the dressing: In a small mixing bowl, whisk together the Kalamata brine with the Dijon, then drizzle in the olive oil while continuing to whisk.

2. Make the salad: In a large mixing bowl, toss the greens with half of the dressing. Transfer to a large serving platter, scattered throughout the platter nicely.

3. On top of the salad, either scatter or put in little piles the olives, mushrooms, mozzarella, Parmesan, artichokes, tomatoes, salami, pear slices, and croutons — and any variations or additions you choose to use.

4. Drizzle the balsamic glaze over the top. Then drizzle the rest of the dressing over the top as well, and end with a sprinkling of the torn basil leaves.

Salad—Hawaiian Macaroni Salad

Once you've had this Hawaiian macaroni salad, that's it — you're hooked for life! No more "non-Hawaiian macaroni salad" ever again. Yes, it's a popular dish at our favorite Island destination, and it will certainly be crowned the most popular dish on your pool party buffet. What's so great and different about it? It's the creamy, tangy, sweet, vinegary flavor, along with the addition of onion, ham, and cucumbers. Serve in a large bowl or in little pre-portioned cups to make for more of a grab-and-go (and jump in the pool) vibe. Aloha!

- [ ] 8 oz. elbow macaroni
- [ ] 4 t. olive oil
- [ ] 8 T. mayonnaise
- [ ] 3 T. rice wine vinegar
- [ ] 3 ½ t. sugar
- [ ] 1 white onion, diced
- [ ] 4 Persian cucumbers, chopped
- [ ] 8 slices ham, chopped
- [ ] 4 hard-boiled eggs, chopped
- [ ] Kosher salt
- [ ] Black pepper
- [ ] 1 c. green onions, sliced

1. Make the dressing: In a small mixing bowl, combine the mayonnaise, 1 tablespoon of the vinegar, and 1 ½ teaspoons of the sugar. Set aside.

2. Prep the macaroni: In a large pot, boil 12 cups of water. Once boiling, add 1 tablespoon of salt and the macaroni. Cook according to the package directions. Once done, drain and transfer the macaroni to a large bowl. Add the olive oil, 2 tablespoons of the vinegar, and 2 teaspoons of the sugar, and stir well. Let cool completely.

3. When the macaroni is cooled, put the salad together: Stir in the onion, cucumber, and ham. Mix well.

4. Stir in the egg, the mayonnaise dressing, 2 teaspoons salt, and a few turns of fresh black pepper. Mix well.

5. Chill the salad in the refrigerator for about 1 hour before serving. Just before serving, sprinkle chopped green onions on the top.

Side—BBQ Beans with Turkey Bacon

Since we're going with a good ol' fashioned summer barbecue theme, it's imperative to add a fresh and delicious version of the classic summer dish, BBQ beans. Though I have many BBQ bean recipes in my arsenal, I really love this particular version — it's definitely maple-Dijon forward (a good thing!), and the turkey bacon is a great addition. Plus, this recipe is super-easy to prepare. You can make it in advance and just reheat when ready. You'll evoke all kinds of good vibes and feels of summer BBQs and picnics of yesteryear.

- ☐ Coconut oil
- ☐ 6 slices turkey bacon, chopped
- ☐ 1 white onion, chopped
- ☐ 3 garlic cloves, minced
- ☐ 2 t. chopped fresh thyme
- ☐ 2 15-oz. cans white beans (cannellini or Great Northern), drained and rinsed
- ☐ ⅓ c. ketchup
- ☐ ⅓ c. maple syrup
- ☐ 2 T. Dijon mustard
- ☐ 1 T. apple cider vinegar
- ☐ ½ t. black pepper

1. In a large skillet, heat a few tablespoons of coconut oil. Add the bacon, onion, garlic, and thyme, cooking over medium-high heat for about 5 minutes. The bacon should be browned and onions softened.

2. Add the beans, ketchup, syrup, mustard, vinegar, pepper, and 1½ cups water. Let simmer over medium-low heat until well thickened, about 20 minutes.

Main—Grilled Chicken Cobb Salad

For the entrée section of your pool party menu, I say let's fire up the grill. Why? Because this recipe is super-flavorful, and is also just a great recipe for cooking up some chicken, whether paired with a salad or not. And this dressing will be one you'll return to again and again. All in all, it's a poolside beauty.

- ☐ 1–2 lbs. boneless chicken breast strips
- ☐ 1 small onion, sliced into ½-in. thick rings
- ☐ 1 c. buttermilk
- ☐ 2 cloves garlic, minced
- ☐ ¾ t. Kosher salt
- ☐ ¾ t. black pepper
- ☐ 6 slices bacon
- ☐ 1 egg
- ☐ ¼ c. vegetable oil
- ☐ 4 t. white wine vinegar
- ☐ 1 T. Dijon mustard
- ☐ 2 hearts of romaine, chopped
- ☐ 1 tomato, chopped
- ☐ 2 avocados, chopped
- ☐ ½ c. blue cheese, crumbled
- ☐ 3 hard-boiled eggs, chopped
- ☐ Bacon bits, for garnish

1. In a large bowl, combine the chicken strips, onion slices, ¾ cup of the buttermilk, garlic, and ½ teaspoon each of salt and pepper. Stir together and let sit in the refrigerator for 1 to 2 hours.

2. Cook the bacon slices over medium heat, turning until crispy. Place on a paper towel–lined plate. Once cool, chop into little pieces. Reserve the grease in the pan.

3. Bring a small saucepan of water to a boil and add the uncooked egg. Let it cook for 4 minutes, then remove from the water. Set it aside to cool.

4. For the dressing, place the cooled 4-minute egg into a blender, then add the oil, reserved bacon grease, remaining ¼ c. buttermilk, vinegar, mustard, ¼ teaspoon salt, and ¼ teaspoon pepper. Blend until smooth and slightly thick, about 1 minute. Set aside.

5. Set the grill to medium heat and spray with cooking spray. Place the chicken strips on the grill and lightly season with salt and pepper. Grill the chicken strips, turning once, until cooked through, about 8 minutes. Grill the onion slices, flipping as needed, until soft and slightly blackened. Chop the onions into little pieces.

6. In a large salad bowl, toss the romaine, onions, tomatoes, avocados, blue cheese, and ¼ cup of the dressing. Place the salad on a large serving platter and top with the chicken, bacon bits, and chopped eggs. Drizzle with the remaining dressing and lightly season with fresh black pepper.

Main—Grilled Turkey-Apple Burgers

Well, it's a pool party after all, so it's a no-brainer to grill up a burger. And why not a beautiful, vibrant, and healthy turkey burger? This recipe is one I've been cooking for decades now. The additions of apples, green onions, lemon, parsley, and the key ingredient — mango chutney — make for a moist and flavorful bite of goodness. Your pool party revelers will be ecstatic.

- ☐ ¼ c. green onions, thinly sliced
- ☐ 3 green apples, peeled and diced
- ☐ 2 T. olive oil
- ☐ 3 lbs. ground turkey
- ☐ 2 T. salt
- ☐ 1 T. pepper
- ☐ 2 t. hot sauce
- ☐ Juice and zest of 1 lemon
- ☐ 1 c. parsley, chopped
- ☐ ½ c. mango chutney
- ☐ 8 hamburger buns or rolls of your choice (toasted or not — I like to spray with coconut oil, season with smoked paprika, and place on the grill for about 1 minute)
- ☐ 1 c. mayonnaise
- ☐ Arugula leaves

1. In a small saucepan, sauté the green onions and diced apple in the olive oil until softened.
2. In a large mixing bowl, combine the ground turkey, salt, pepper, hot sauce, lemon juice and zest, parsley, ¼ cup of the chutney, and the sauteed apples and onions. Mix well with your hands.
3. Shape into 8 patties and let them sit in the refrigerator for up to 2 hours.
4. When ready to grill, season the patties with salt and pepper. Grill on a lightly oiled grill, about 7 minutes on each side, or until cooked through.
5. Let the patties sit for about 5 minutes. While sitting, stir together the mayonnaise and the remaining ¼ cup of chutney in a small bowl.
6. To assemble, spread some of the mayo on the bottom bun. Add the patty. Place some arugula leaves on top, and top with the other half of the bun. (If you want, spread a bit of the mayo on this side as well.)
7. Cut the burgers in half and serve on a large platter.

Dessert—Chocolate Cold Brew Pistachio Cake Cups

For your pool party desserts, I'm presenting two different variations of "dessert in a cup." This first one is a great outdoor party addition: decadent chunks of coffee-infused chocolate goodness cake, topped with a creamy and rich mascarpone-infused pistachio frosting. How could it get any better?

Cake
- ☐ 1 c. flour
- ☐ ¾ c. sugar
- ☐ ½ c. cocoa powder
- ☐ ¾ t. baking powder
- ☐ ½ t. baking soda
- ☐ ½ t. Kosher salt
- ☐ ½ c. buttermilk
- ☐ ¼ c. vegetable oil
- ☐ 1 t. vanilla extract
- ☐ 1 egg
- ☐ 6 T. cold brew coffee

Frosting
- ☐ ½ c. butter, softened
- ☐ 8 oz. mascarpone cheese, softened
- ☐ 3 c. powdered sugar
- ☐ Zest of 1 lemon
- ☐ 1 t. vanilla extract
- ☐ ½ t. almond extract
- ☐ ⅓ c. chopped pistachios, plus more for garnish
- ☐ Whipped cream, for garnish

1. Bake the cake: Preheat the oven to 350 degrees. Grease and line a 9 x 13-inch baking dish with parchment paper.

2. In a large bowl, whisk together the flour, sugar, cocoa powder, baking powder, baking soda, and salt.

3. In a medium bowl, whisk together the buttermilk, oil, vanilla, and egg. Combine the wet and dry ingredients, mixing well. Stir in the coffee.

4. Pour the batter into the prepared pan and bake for about 20 minutes. The center will not be jiggly. Let the cake cool completely in the pan and then remove to a plate.

5. Make the frosting: In a medium bowl, mix together the butter, mascarpone, powdered sugar, the lemon zest, and a pinch of salt until well combined. Add the vanilla and almond extracts, mixing well. Stir in the chopped pistachios.

6. Assemble the cups: Using your hands, crumble the cake into small chunks. Place some chunks of the cake into small serving cups, slightly pressing down. Put a dollop of frosting on top. Add more cake chunks and top with more frosting, spreading to cover the cake. Put a dollop of whipped cream on top of each cake cup, and a few pistachios as well.

Dessert—Pretzel Salad Cups

I love, love, love me some pretzel salad! Yeah, it's not really a salad, but rather a dessert that combines both sweet and salty notes, along with a few contrasting textures. Here those textures are in the form of a cream cheese layer, and then...a Jello layer! I like to play up the summer vibe by using peach gelatin and peach slices. The bright orange gelatin layer is beautiful and resembles that other pool party mainstay, an Aperol spritz. It's unique, totally summery, and deee-lish!

- [ ] 2 c. crushed pretzels
- [ ] 4 T. butter, melted
- [ ] 3 T. sugar
- [ ] 1 8-oz. package cream cheese, softened
- [ ] 8 oz. frozen whipped topping, plus some for garnish
- [ ] ¾ c. powdered sugar
- [ ] 1 6-oz. box of Jello, flavor of your choosing (I like to use peach)
- [ ] 2 c. fresh peach slices, plus some chopped pieces for garnish
- [ ] 1 8-oz. can crushed pineapple

1. Preheat the oven to 375 degrees. In a large mixing bowl, combine the crushed pretzels, melted butter, and sugar. Spread the mixture on a baking sheet and bake for about 10 minutes, or until golden brown.
2. Remove the pretzel mixture from the oven and spoon a layer into the bottom of 6 small serving cups.
3. In a medium mixing bowl, beat the cream cheese, whipped topping, and powdered sugar until velvety smooth. Spread a layer of this cream cheese mixture over the pretzel mixture in the 6 serving cups.
4. In another medium bowl, dissolve the Jello in 2 cups of boiling water. Allow the gelatin to cool completely. Once cooled, stir in the peach slices and crushed pineapple. Spread a layer of the gelatin on top of the cream cheese layer.
5. Cover the serving cups with plastic wrap and allow the parfaits to set in the refrigerator until well set, about 3 hours.
6. Before serving, garnish each cup with a spoonful of whipped topping and the reserved peach chunks on top.

NOT YOUR AVERAGE SHOWER!

Let's plan a baby shower! Or a wedding shower! Or any type of shower!

I love planning these — it's great to take a party that traditionally has been thrown one way (as a gathering of a bunch of girls…no drinks…same old games), and turning it on its head and doing it a different, fresh way. When my partner and I were adopting our kids, our friends threw us a wild baby shower that I've always tried to emulate and top whenever I've planned these events since then.

The goal here is to celebrate the occasion but to have something for everyone. This includes, of course, a cocktail, as well as a good mocktail, and a table full of either finger foods or foods put into plastic cups or cute glassware or jars. The whole event must be very low-maintenance, so when the party starts you don't really need to do anything but have fun.

For this menu I include one staple — a lovely fluffy coconut-cilantro rice — with two different entrée options that you can easily layer into a small jar, or you can create a build-your-own jar station. And if you are throwing a baby shower…well, you can't go wrong with pickle finger sandwiches!

PARTY GAMES

For a baby shower there are countless games out there. I like these, since they seem to generate the most laughs and adult-camaraderie.

- **Onesie Decorating:** Give everyone a plain white onesie and fabric pens, then have a timed onesie decorating contest. The parent(s)-to-be is the judge.
- **Balloon Popping:** Put everyone in teams and give each team member an uninflated balloon. Each team member must blow up the balloon, tie it, and put it under their shirt. Once the team is finished with this step, everyone must try to pop all of the balloons without using any hands. The first team to pop all of them wins!
- **"Name that Baby Tune":** Make a playlist of baby-related songs. Divide guests into teams. Play each song until one person correctly identifies the name of the song. Keep score and award prizes.

Drinks—Sublime Sangria (Boozy and Not Boozy)

Sangria makes a perfect liquid complement to a baby or bridal shower. You can make it in a big jug the day before and just refill the pitcher as needed during the party. My go-to fruit additions are peaches and berries, but you can use any fruit here. And for the non-alcoholic version, I like to make a similar type of fruit-soaked mocktail, giving the mom-to-be or teetotalers their own version of the classic party drink. For both, add the seltzer or soda at the last minute to up the effervescence factor!

Boozy Sangria
Fills a pitcher or about 6 glasses

- ☐ 1 750-ml. bottle rosé wine
- ☐ ⅓ c. berry liqueur such as Chambord or Framboise
- ☐ 1 T. sugar
- ☐ 2 ½ c. sliced peaches
- ☐ 1 c. blackberries
- ☐ 1 c. lemon-lime soda

1. In a large pitcher, stir together the wine, liqueur, and sugar.
2. Add the fruit and then refrigerate the mixture for a minimum of 4 hours. (I refrigerate it overnight.)
3. Before serving, add the lemon-lime soda.
4. Serve in the pitcher next to an ice bucket (don't add ice to the pitcher). Set some punch glasses or wine glasses next to the pitcher with a few ice cubes and few blackberries in them, ready for the addition of sangria!

Mocktail Sangria
Fills a pitcher or about 6 glasses

- ☐ 3 c. cranberry juice
- ☐ ½ c. orange juice
- ☐ 1 can plain club soda or seltzer water
- ☐ Thinly sliced fruit such as oranges, pears, and apples (up to 1 each)
- ☐ ¼ c. finely sliced basil leaves

1. In a large pitcher, stir together the liquids.
2. Add the fruit slices and basil.
3. As with the sangria, serve in the pitcher next to an ice bucket (don't add ice to the pitcher). Set some glasses next to the pitcher with ice and a few fruit slices in them.

Appy—Cheesy Olive Puffs

Of all the foods you put on the table for this party, this is the dish people will grab by the handful until it is gone. Full of cheesy and salty olive-y goodness, these olives are the perfect appetizer. You will certainly impress your guests with these ultra-easy "baked goods," and you can make them in advance and freeze them as well. They are great for all types of parties, but I think they go really well with this finger foods–style event.

- ☐ 2 c. shredded mild cheddar cheese (or you can use a blend of cheddars)
- ☐ 8 T. (1 stick) salted butter, at room temperature
- ☐ 1 c. flour
- ☐ 1 t. hot sauce
- ☐ 1 clove garlic, minced
- ☐ 1 jar (5 oz.) of pimiento-stuffed green olives (about 3 dozen)

1. Place the cheese and softened butter in a food processor and mix until just combined.
2. Add the flour, hot sauce, and garlic, and blend until well combined.
3. Form the dough into a ball, cover with plastic wrap, and refrigerate for at least 1 hour. The dough should be firm.
4. Preheat the oven to 350 degrees.
5. Break off a small golf ball–sized piece of dough, flatten it with your fingers, and place an olive in the middle. Using your fingers, cover the olive completely with the dough. Do this with all the olives and dough.
6. Place each dough ball onto a baking sheet about 1 inch apart.
7. Bake for about 15 minutes, or until golden brown.
8. Let cool on a wire rack, then serve!

Salad—Delectable Curry Chicken Salad

I'm a curry fanatic and gravitate toward anything in the curry-tinged world. And curry chicken salad is probably at the top of the list. This easy and oh-so-good recipe for curry chicken salad can be used for sandwiches (hot or grilled), eaten directly out of a bowl with a fork, or in this manner — served alongside crackers, cucumbers, or even lettuce wrap leaves. I've yet to host a party where this wasn't devoured. I often make this salad on Sundays to have for my lunch throughout the week. It's that great.

- ☐ 4 T. mayonnaise
- ☐ Zest and juice of ½ lime
- ☐ 2 t. curry powder
- ☐ ¼ t. turmeric
- ☐ 1 clove garlic, minced
- ☐ ½ t. kosher salt
- ☐ ½ t. cayenne pepper
- ☐ 2 cooked chicken breasts, shredded
- ☐ 2 T. chopped cilantro leaves
- ☐ Crackers, for serving
- ☐ Cucumber slices, for serving

1. In a large mixing bowl, combine all ingredients except for the chicken and cilantro leaves and mix well.
2. Place the chicken in a bowl and mix in the curry mayonnaise sauce gradually to get to your desired consistency.
3. Stir in the cilantro leaves.
4. Serve in a small serving bowl with crackers and cucumbers on the side, along with lettuce wrap leaves if you so desire.

Side—Your New Favorite Coconut-Cilantro Rice

For years I avoided making rice — especially because I could simply buy frozen bags of brown, white, or Jasmine rice and heat them up in the microwave. I was always afraid of the process — of burning it, undercooking it, and any number of other unfortunate outcomes — until I discovered how stupidly easy it is to make!

I pretty much always make rice the same way now — soaked in coconut milk with a handful of herbs (here I use cilantro) and some lime (and sometimes lemon) juice stirred in at the end. It's a no-brainer! I now make it several times a week as a complement to nearly anything.

For this party, I suggest making a batch of this delectable rice and serving it with the two entrées listed in this chapter. You can put it in a nice serving dish on the food table with both entrées, where guests can self-serve, or pre-dish it all into little mason jars or glasses or cups with rice on the bottom and entrée on top. Your choice!

- ☐ 2 c. uncooked Jasmine rice
- ☐ 2 15-oz. cans coconut milk
- ☐ ½ c. water
- ☐ ¼ t. salt
- ☐ ¼ c. finely chopped cilantro
- ☐ Juice of 1 lime

1. Combine the rice, coconut milk, water, and salt in a large saucepan and bring to a boil.
2. Once boiling starts, turn the heat to low and cover the saucepan. Let sit for 15 minutes.
3. Remove from heat and let sit, still covered, for another 10 minutes.
4. Remove the lid and stir in the cilantro and lime juice. Mix well.

Side—Cup o' Grapes Fruit Salad

You *must* include a fruit side at a shower, and no one wants an old-school bowl of fruit sitting around. I've freshened up the concept with this delightful little cup of joy — grapes and berries tossed in a minty vanilla fresh yogurt dressing. Serve the fruit in little jars or cups. For a baby shower, how about in sippy cups? Either way, it's a winner.

- ☐ 1 c. vanilla yogurt
- ☐ 2 oz. cream cheese, softened
- ☐ 1 T. honey
- ☐ ½ t. cinnamon
- ☐ ½ t. finely chopped fresh mint
- ☐ 6 c. seedless red and green grapes, halved
- ☐ 2 c. blackberries

1. To create the dressing, mix the yogurt, cream cheese, honey, cinnamon, and mint in a blender until smooth.

2. In a mixing bowl, combine the grapes and blackberries with the dressing. Coat the fruit well.

3. Refrigerate until ready to serve.

4. To serve, I suggest portioning the fruit into little plastic cups, sippy cups, champagne flutes, or mason jars.

Main—Pickle-Craving Finger Sandwiches

Any solid baby or bridal shower needs some finger sandwiches. And what about those pickle cravings? (I have them all the time, and I'm not with child.) My family has made these sandwiches for years — basically, we put pickles seasoned a few different ways and some good sharp cheddar on toasted bread. Make them for this party and also keep them in mind for future picnics and packed lunches. This recipe makes two finger sandwiches (one full sandwich cut in half diagonally — you can adjust to make as many finger sandwiches as you need.

- ☐ 1 T. finely diced dill pickles
- ☐ 1 T. mayonnaise
- ☐ 1 t. whole-grain Dijon mustard
- ☐ ½ t. pickle brine
- ☐ A few leaves of fresh tarragon, thinly sliced
- ☐ A few leaves of fresh baby spinach
- ☐ 1 dill pickle, thinly sliced (sandwich slices)
- ☐ 1 slice sharp cheddar cheese
- ☐ 2 slices seedy bread, lightly toasted

1. In a small mixing bowl, combine the diced pickle, mayonnaise, mustard, and pickle brine, and mix well to create a sauce.
2. Spread a layer of sauce on each slice of bread.
3. On one of the bread slices, place the tarragon leaves and spinach leaves on top of the sauce.
4. Add the sliced pickle, creating one full layer of thinly sliced pickle.
5. Cover with a cheese slice.
6. Close the sandwich with the second slice of bread, and then cut diagonally to create cute little finger sandwiches.

Main—Tasty Turkey Picadillo Cups

I have been writing a weekly food blog for the past year, posting new recipes every week. By far one of my post popular posts has been the recipe for my picadillo enchiladas. Of course, before actually creating the enchiladas, you first make a batch of this amazing picadillo. It is usually made with ground beef — and it's so good I just want to stand at the stove and devour it from the pan with a fork! You can also make batches and freeze it. In addition to enchiladas, it goes great over rice, with chips, in a tortilla — your choice.

For this party, I suggest you pair this delectable dish with Your New Favorite Coconut-Cilantro Rice and serve it in cute little jars, or set up a self-serve station on your buffet table. I used turkey in this recipe to lighten it up a bit and put a new twist on it. I guarantee this picadillo masterpiece, with its mix of sweet golden raisins, olives, and capers, will be a crowd pleaser!

- ☐ 2 T. vegetable oil
- ☐ 1 white onion, diced
- ☐ 1 garlic clove, minced
- ☐ 1 bell pepper (any color), diced
- ☐ 1 lb. ground turkey
- ☐ 1 t. kosher salt
- ☐ 1 t. black pepper
- ☐ 1 t. Chinese five-spice seasoning
- ☐ 1 14-oz. can tomato sauce
- ☐ 1 T. capers
- ☐ ½ c. sliced green olives
- ☐ ¼ c. golden raisins

1. In a large skillet over medium heat, warm up a few tablespoons of oil. Add the onion, garlic, and bell pepper. Let it soften up, about 5 minutes.
2. Stir in the turkey, salt, pepper, and Chinese five-spice seasoning.
3. Cook, stirring until the meat browns, about 5 minutes.
4. Stir in the tomato sauce, capers, olives, and raisins. Let this all cook together for about 5 minutes — it should thicken up nicely. If needed, add salt and pepper to taste.
5. To serve, layer it in little jars or glasses with a large serving of the rice on the bottom and the picadillo on top. Or, set up a self-service station on the party food table.

Main—Tiny Thai Basil Beef Bowls

For a second entrée to pair with your New Favorite Coconut-Cilantro Rice, you can't go wrong with this simple and oh-so-good Thai basil beef recipe. If you like Thai food, this is a pretty standard recipe found on many Thai menus. It is super easy and super tasty — and it's great paired with the fluffy coconut rice. I'd take a little bowl or jar, put a scoop of rice on the bottom, pile on a nice helping of this Thai basil beef, and then throw on top a few of the soy-marinated cukes. May I have seconds, please?

- ☐ 2 Persian cucumbers, cut into little stalks
- ☐ ¾ cup + 1 t. soy sauce
- ☐ 1 c. fresh basil, chopped
- ☐ Juice of 2 limes
- ☐ 1 t. sugar
- ☐ 2 T. vegetable oil
- ☐ 1 lb. ground beef
- ☐ 1 red bell pepper, diced
- ☐ 4 green onions, finely sliced
- ☐ 1 jalapeno, diced
- ☐ 3 cloves garlic, minced
- ☐ Coconut-cilantro rice (see page 97 earlier in this menu)

1. In a small mixing bowl, toss the cucumber stalks with 1 teaspoon of the soy sauce and 1 tablespoon of the basil. Set aside.
2. In another small bowl, whisk together ¼ cup of the soy sauce, the lime juice, and sugar. Set aside.
3. In a medium skillet, heat 1 tablespoon of the oil over high heat. Add the ground beef and cook, breaking up the meat, until cooked through, about 5 minutes. Remove the beef and set aside.
4. In the same skillet, add the second tablespoon of oil over medium heat. Add the bell pepper, green onions, and jalapenos, cooking until softened, about 4 minutes. Add the garlic and cook well for a few minutes more.
5. Increase the heat to high and mix in the beef and soy sauce mixture. Cook until the liquid evaporates, about 3 minutes. Add the remaining basil and stir until the basil wilts, about 1 minute.
6. To serve, layer it in little bowls or jars with a layer of the coconut-cilantro rice on the bottom and a scoop of the Thai Beef on top, garnished with a few cucumbers. Or set up a self-service station on the party food table.

Dessert—Lovely and Lemony Olive Oil Cake

Any chance I get to use fresh lemons from our tree, I'm all in. And there's not a cake out there better than this moist, decadent, and luxuriously lemony olive oil cake. The frosting alone is so unique and surprising with creamy notes of sour cream and pineapple preserves. I make this all the time, delivering it to friends for birthdays. Often they tell me it's the best cake they've ever had — and it makes the perfect sweet addition to the perfect baby or bridal shower. YUM!

Cake
- ☐ 1 ½ c. flour
- ☐ ½ c. almond flour
- ☐ 1 t. kosher salt
- ☐ 1 t. baking soda
- ☐ 1 t. baking powder
- ☐ Zest of 1 lemon
- ☐ ¾ c. plain Greek yogurt
- ☐ Juice of 1 lemon (about ¼ cup)
- ☐ 2 eggs
- ☐ ¾ c. olive oil
- ☐ 1 ¼ c. sugar
- ☐ 1 t. almond extract

Fluffy Pineapple Frosting
- ☐ 1 c. pineapple marmalade (or other fruit preserves)
- ☐ ¾ c. heavy cream
- ☐ 3 T. sugar
- ☐ ¾ c. sour cream
- ☐ Colored sprinkles, for garnish

1. Preheat the oven to 350 degrees. Generously grease one 9-inch round cake pan and line it with parchment paper.
2. In a medium mixing bowl, whisk together the flour, almond flour, salt, baking soda, and bakng powder. Stir in the lemon zest.
3. In a small bowl, mix together the yogurt and lemon juice. Set aside.
4. In a large mixing bowl, combine the eggs, olive oil, and sugar. Stir in the almond extract.
5. Mix the ingredients in all three bowls together to create a batter.
6. Pour the batter into the prepared pan and bake for 40 minutes, or until the cake is well set. Let it cool for a few minutes, then remove the cake from the pan using the parchment paper and let it cool completely.
7. Make the frosting: In a small saucepan, warm the pineapple marmalade over low heat until it is soft and spreadable. Let cool.
8. In a mixing bowl, beat the heavy cream until soft peaks form. Add the sugar and beat for 1 minute, or until stiff peaks form.
9. Fold in the marmalade and sour cream.
10. Frost the cake. There's no need for perfection — make it a bit rustic looking! Top with whatever sprinkles you have in your cupboard!

Dessert—Lemon-Lime Chiffon Pie, Oh My!

As an alternative, or a complement, to your olive oil cake, I recommend this crowd-pleaser of a pie. It's basically a key lime pie with a salty saltine crust and a fluffy and delicious lemon-tinted whipped topping. Oh, and some more salt flakes on top. Perfect for a daytime event or a shower like this one! I've made this for more barbecues, parties, and showers than I can remember — and it's always a hit!

- ☐ 1 ½ c. finely crushed saltine crackers
- ☐ 6 T. unsalted butter, melted
- ☐ 3 T. sugar
- ☐ 1 egg white, lightly beaten
- ☐ 1 14-oz. can sweetened condensed milk
- ☐ 4 egg yolks
- ☐ Juice of 2 limes (about ¼ cup)
- ☐ 1 ½ c. heavy whipping cream
- ☐ ¼ c. powdered sugar
- ☐ Zest of 1 lemon
- ☐ Lime zest, for garnish
- ☐ Maldon sea salt flakes, for garnish

1. Preheat the oven to 350 degrees. In a medium mixing bowl, combine the crushed crackers, melted butter, sugar, and egg white until well combined.
2. Press the crust mix into a 9-inch glass pie dish, pressing down firmly on the bottom and up the sides. Place in the freezer for 10 minutes.
3. Remove from the freezer and bake until lightly browned, about 20 minutes. Let cool slightly.
4. Make the filling: In a medium mixing bowl, whisk together the condensed milk and egg yolks until smooth. Whisk in the lime juice. Pour this mixture onto the slightly warm crust.
5. Bake until the center is just set, about 15 minutes. Let cool, and then chill in refrigerator for at least 2 hours.
6. For the whipped topping, beat the heavy cream and powdered sugar with an electric mixer on high until stiff peaks form, about 3 minutes. Stir in the lemon zest.
7. Spread the topping over the chilled pie, leaving the crust slightly visible. Garnish with a dusting of lime zest and a light sprinkling of sea salt flakes.

AWARDS SHOW PARTY!

Let's be real. I've probably been hosting Oscars parties since I was 10. Every year. Cooking all the food, organizing the ballots, contests, and games — it's something I'm known for in my world. I know not everyone is that gung-ho about movie awards shows. But what about getting friends together for the Grammys? Country Music Awards? Hell, Election Night? Just grab your posse, cook up some great food, throw it all onto a buffet table, have some contests and games, and you've got a party on your hands.

Do I theme the food to tie to the Oscars? You know I have. But lately I've shied away from that and have just put out some great eats. I'm not suggesting you cook all these dishes for any given party — unless it's a huge one. Think of this chapter as a Choose-Your-Own-Award-Night-Menu Adventure. I suggest making Da Bomb BBQ Sauce, and using it two ways: with the Panko-Breaded Chicken Strips as a dipper, and also on the Western Sliders as a sauce. And yes, make both desserts. Why not? It's a party!

PARTY GAMES

Regardless of what the show is, you should definitely have a contest with a ballot. For the Oscars, one thing I like to do is find short scripted scenes from the nominated films (they are often available online), and each time that film is introduced throughout the show, draw names of your guests out of a hat to re-enact the scene. So fun. Also, for those who aren't as great with the predictions, have fun prizes for the worst score — it's been an annual tradition of mine to award a mega-container of cheesy puffs. (My friends have vied for the worst score just to get this!) And of course, Oscar Bingo is always a hit — just get blank bingo cards online and add all the movies and actors nominated to the squares. Whenever that name is read, mark your card. You know the drill.

Drinks—Pimm's Cups and Strawberry Bubblies

Those who know me know that my favorite cocktail — like ever — is a Pimm's Cup. What is Pimm's? It's a gin-based spirit. To me, a Pimm's Cup is like drinking an adult iced tea. I first experienced these little glasses of yummy when I was studying law in England. Someone ordered one for me at a pub and I was hooked. I've been making them ever since. Pimm's Cups are also popular in the American South, with the largest difference being, apparently, the amount of fruit added, and whether it also includes ginger ale. That being said, it's the perfect party drink. I like to make it in a pitcher and set up a self-service station for guests to add however much mint, cucumbers, strawberries, and lemons they want. And since this recipe is for an Oscars (or not) party, I had to also include a bubbly option. What's better than a tall wine glass full of champagne and strawberries on ice? Choose one of these libations or the other — or both. Your guests will be thrilled either way.

Pitcher of Pimm's Cups

Makes one pitcher, or about 4 or 5 glasses.

- ☐ 18 oz. Pimm's No. 1
- ☐ 1 oz. lemonade (store-bought)
- ☐ 12 oz. spicy ginger ale (or ginger beer)
- ☐ 2 Persian cucumbers, sliced
- ☐ 6 strawberries, sliced
- ☐ 12 fresh mint leaves, sliced
- ☐ 2 lemons, sliced

1. In a large pitcher, stir together the Pimm's, lemonade, and ginger ale. Add a few lemon slices to the pitcher.
2. To serve, set the pitcher next to an ice bucket (don't add ice to the pitcher) and place glasses around the pitcher. Garnish each glass with ice, a few cucumber and strawberry slices, some mint, and a lemon slice. Guests can then fill a glass with the Pimm's mixture.

Strawberry Bubblies

- ☐ 1 c. fresh strawberries, sliced
- ☐ 2 T. sugar
- ☐ 1 t. fresh lemon juice
- ☐ 1 750-ml. bottle sparkling rosé or prosecco

1. In a large bowl, combine the strawberries, sugar, and lemon juice. Cover and let sit in the refrigerator for at least 1 hour.
2. Fill 4 large red wine glasses (or whatever glassware you want to use) halfway with ice. Add a bunch of strawberry slices and top the glass off with the bubbly.
3. You can also make this in a pitcher. Fill a pitcher with the strawberries and champagne, and set next to an ice bucket (don't add ice to the pitcher). Place glasses around the pitcher for guests to serve themselves.

Appy—The Quick(est) and Easy(iest) Amazing Layered Dip

We've all been to parties where someone buys a layered dip from the grocery store and drops it down on the buffet. No shame there, but in the time it takes to do that you could just whip up your own. This one is SO easy and a true crowd pleaser. I love it with "Soyrizo" — a soy-based alternative to chorizo sausage — which you can buy in most grocery stores. Of course, you can substitute the real thing if you so choose. As for the hummus layer, I say go store-bought. However, feel free to whip out the old food processor and easily whip up your own as well.

This is the type of dish you can embellish to your heart's delight, adding such items as sliced black olives, diced jalapenos, green onion — the list goes on. But this is my go-to combo right here. Serve this on your Oscars party buffet along with your favorite tortilla chips. You may want to make a backup even, depending on the number of guests. I've yet to see this dip not get scarfed down, fully.

- ☐ 1 12-oz. package of Soyrizo (or real chorizo)
- ☐ 1 10-oz. container of store-bought hummus
- ☐ 2 avocados, chopped
- ☐ 2 T. fresh lime juice
- ☐ 1 c. pico de gallo salsa
- ☐ 1 c. Mexican crema (or use sour cream slightly watered down with milk or water)
- ☐ ½ c. chopped cilantro
- ☐ Tortilla chips

1. In a skillet over medium heat, break up the Soyrizo and cook until browned and crumbly. Set aside.
2. Layer the ingredients in a glass serving dish (about 9 x 9 inches) or a glass pie pan in the following order:
   - Spread the hummus over the bottom of the dish. On top of that sprinkle the avocados. Next, drizzle the lime juice all over.
   - Next, sprinkle ⅔ of the Soyrizo crumbles over the top. Spread the pico de gallo over the Soyrizo. Then drizzle over that ½ cup of the crema.
   - Sprinkle with the cilantro and then cover with the remaining Soyrizo crumbles. Drizzle with the remaining crema over the top.
3. Serve with tortilla chips.

Appy—Greek Pita Walking Taco Snack Bags

Ever had Frito Pie in a Bag? Or gone to a fair and enjoyed a "walking taco"? Walking tacos are snack-sized bags of chips, opened at the top, with a bunch of taco ingredients added to the top that you can eat with a fork while walking around. Super fun. I've tried to elevate these over the years with random toppings, so for this Oscars (or other) party, I decided to make one Greek-style over a snack bag of pita chips. These snack bags are really fun if you have kids coming to the party — or no kids, and you just want something fun and kitschy on the table that tastes great as well. This dish will really give your guests something to talk about!

- ☐ 8 1.5-oz. snack bags of pita chips
- ☐ 1 lb. ground beef (or turkey or plant-based meat)
- ☐ 1 t. garlic salt
- ☐ 2 t. Greek seasoning (or use dried oregano, salt, and pepper)
- ☐ ½ c. store-bought hummus
- ☐ ¼ c. plain yogurt
- ☐ 2 Persian cucumbers, chopped
- ☐ 1 c. cherry tomatoes, halved
- ☐ ½ c. Kalamata olives, chopped
- ☐ 4 oz. crumbled feta cheese

1. In a large skillet, brown the beef with the garlic salt and Greek seasoning. Drain and set aside.

2. In a small mixing bowl, whisk together the hummus, yogurt, and 2 tablespoons water. Set aside.

3. Carefully cut the tops off the pita chips bags and display the bags all standing up next to each other, open at the top.

4. Put a large serving spoonful of the meat on top of the chips.

5. Over the meat mixture, layer some cucumber pieces, tomatoes, olives, and feta.

6. Drizzle the hummus yogurt sauce on top of the mixture.

7. Place on a large platter and serve.

Salad—Alluring Arugula Pear Salad

So you have to throw a salad in here. I shared the recipes for many of my favorite go-to salads in the original *A Perfect 10* cookbook — and any would work at this party — but here's a simple and fresh one to add to the roster. It's so easy and basic — really only four ingredients — but it sure packs a flavor punch. As with other buffet-style parties, you can serve this in a large salad bowl with little bowls or cups arranged next to it. I often put a serving of salad into small cups and set them on the buffet, ready to be picked up, carried around, and enjoyed. Your choice.

- ☐ 1 15-oz. can pear halves, drained (but reserve the juice)
- ☐ 2 T. basic vinaigrette (recipe below)
- ☐ 2 c. baby arugula
- ☐ ½ c. gorgonzola crumbles
- ☐ 4 T. glazed pecans

1. In a large bowl, whisk together 2 tablespoons of the pear juice with the vinaigrette dressing. Season to taste with salt and pepper.
2. Add the arugula, gorgonzola, pears, and pecans, and toss well to coat.
3. Serve either pre-set in little punch cups, or at a self-service station in a large salad bowl with little bowls or cups.

Basic Vinaigrette

- ☐ ¼ c. white wine vinegar
- ☐ ¾ c. olive oil (or any other oil you want to use here)

1. Whisk all ingredients together in a mixing bowl (or do what I do and put them in a mason jar and shake, shake, shake). That's it.

Main—Mouthwatering Chicken Mole Tostadas

For a buffet-style party, a slow cooker can be your greatest ally. The morning of your party, just throw these ingredients into the cooker, cook low and slow for 6 hours, and that's about it — you will have tasty shredded chicken in a simple mole-style sauce, ready to put into tacos or a tostada. For this party, I suggest setting up a self-service tostada station, putting the slow cooker right on the buffet, plugged-in on warm only, along with tostada shells and an array of condiments. This self-service station will allow your guests to get creative and make the ideal tostada for their tastes. Make sure you start with my homemade Tim's Refried Beans as the first layer (recipe found in *A Perfect 10* cookbook) — they are amazing, and essential to a great tostada!

- ☐ 1 15-oz. can fire-roasted diced tomatoes
- ☐ 1 carrot, chopped
- ☐ 1 green bell pepper, chopped
- ☐ 3 green onions, chopped
- ☐ ½ c. chopped cilantro
- ☐ 3 T. peanut butter (or almond butter)
- ☐ 1 T. chili powder
- ☐ 2 t. unsweetened cocoa powder
- ☐ 3 T. soy sauce
- ☐ 2 lbs. boneless chicken breasts
- ☐ 12 store-bought cooked tostada shells
- ☐ For garnishes: crema, shredded lettuce, chopped cilantro, chopped green onions, hot sauce

1. Add all ingredients except the tostada shells and garnishes to a slow cooker and give a stir. Cook on low setting for 6 hours. When the time is up, remove the chicken and use two forks to shred.

2. While the chicken is out of the cooker, either use an immersion blender to blend the ingredients together in the cooker, or use a blender to create a creamy quasi-mole sauce and return to the cooker.

3. Add the shredded chicken back with the sauce and combine well.

4. To serve, place the slow cooker on the food table next to a bowl of Tim's Refried Beans, the tostada shells, and small bowls of garnishes. Have a bottle of hot sauce on hand as well. You can also put out some crema — either store bought, or add about 1 tablespoon or so of water to ½ cup of sour cream to make a creamy sauce. Even add a bit of lime juice if you want!

Main—Can't-Eat-Just-One Western Sliders

Sliders are perfect for many types of parties. They're easy to grab and eat while standing, and easy to make in advance. So throw a platter of these cute little burgers on your party table. Once you make a batch of Da Bomb BBQ Sauce, why not use it two ways: as a zesty sauce on these sliders and as a dip for the Primo Parmesan-Crusted Chicken Strips? And you can do what my mom always did — add crumbled potato chips to the burger too. It's a winner!

- ☐ 1 lb. ground beef
- ☐ 1 t. kosher salt
- ☐ 1 t. black pepper
- ☐ 1 T. Worcestershire sauce
- ☐ 1 c. crushed potato chips
- ☐ 3 shallots, thinly sliced into rounds
- ☐ ¼ c. flour
- ☐ 2 t. cayenne pepper
- ☐ 10 slices cheddar cheese
- ☐ Da Bomb BBQ Sauce (recipe below)
- ☐ 10 slider buns (I like the sweet Hawaiian ones)

1. In a large mixing bowl, combine the ground beef, salt, pepper, and Worcestershire sauce. Mix well. Fold in the potato chips. Form into 10 large golf ball-sized balls, and then press into slider-sized patties.

2. Prepare the shallot rings: Heat about ½ inch of vegetable oil in a large frying pan on medium-high heat. In a small mixing bowl, combine the flour and cayenne. Toss the shallot rings in the mixture, and then place them in a strainer to shake off any excess flour. When the oil is heated, fry the shallots until they are lightly browned. Remove the shallots with a slotted spoon onto a paper towel-lined plate and sprinkle with salt.

3. Cook the burgers: heat the grill and apply cooking spray. Cook each slider for a few minutes on each side, basting with Da Bomb BBQ Sauce. At the last minute, add the cheese and close the lid to melt the cheese. Remove the patties.

4. Lightly toast the inside of the buns.

5. To assemble the sliders, brush the inside of the buns, top and bottom, with Da Bomb BBQ Sauce, mixed with a few tablespoons of mayonnaise. Add the patty and cover with a small smattering of the shallot rings. If desired, add a few dill pickle slices.

6. Pile the sliders onto a platter and place on your party food table!

Da Bomb BBQ Sauce

- ☐ 1 c. yellow mustard
- ☐ ¼ c. Dijon mustard
- ☐ 2 ½ t. hot sauce
- ☐ ¼ t. cayenne pepper
- ☐ 3 T. butter
- ☐ ⅓ c. apple cider vinegar
- ☐ ¾ c. brown sugar
- ☐ 1 t. kosher salt
- ☐ 1 t. black pepper

1. Mix all ingredients in a medium saucepan and simmer on low-medium heat for about 15 minutes, or until thickened. Use right away, or keep in a mason jar in the refrigerator for a few days.

Main—Tantalizing Texas-Style Bean Soup

You may want to have a vegetarian entrée option for this party menu — and this yummy Texas-style bean soup is always a winner. Serve it at a self-service station with mugs for the soup and a bunch of toppings to load up to one's heart's content. It's kind of a cross between chili, tortilla soup, and regular black bean soup. Your guests will love this and will definitely want the recipe. But maybe don't give it to them without a stellar showing on the Oscars contest ballot.

- ☐ 1 T. olive oil
- ☐ 1 white onion, diced
- ☐ 1 garlic clove, minced
- ☐ 1 t. cumin
- ☐ ¼ t. chili powder
- ☐ ½ t. kosher salt
- ☐ ½ t. black pepper
- ☐ 1 15-oz. can diced tomatoes with green chiles
- ☐ 1 15-oz. can pinto beans, not drained
- ☐ 1 15-oz. can black beans, drained
- ☐ 2 c. vegetable stock
- ☐ 1 ½ c. cooked rice (white or brown)
- ☐ ½ c. chopped cilantro
- ☐ 1 c. cheddar cheese, shredded
- ☐ For garnishes: tortilla chips, diced avocados, sliced black olives, sliced jalapenos, hot sauce

1. In a large saucepan over medium heat, heat the olive oil. Add the onions and garlic, and cook, stirring occasionally, for about 5 minutes.

2. Add the cumin, chili powder, salt, and pepper, and cook for about 1 minute. Stir in the tomatoes, both cans of beans, stock, and 4 cups of water. Bring to a boil, then reduce to medium and let simmer for about 15 minutes, stirring occasionally.

3. Remove about 2 cups of the mixture and blend in a blender. Return the mixture to the soup, along with the rice and about ½ of the cilantro. Cook until thickened, about 5 minutes.

4. Serve in a nice serving dish, or even in a slow cooker, alongside tortilla chips and small bowls of garnishes.

Main—Primo Parmesan-Crusted Chicken Strips

Chicken strips are always a winner — and this recipe is a super simple, super tasty way to do it. Crusted with breadcrumbs and parmesan and baked — not fried! Just serve these on a big platter with a few elevated dipping sauces. I recommend my Da Bomb BBQ Sauce (see recipe 6 earlier in this menu) and this amazing Taleggio Cheese Sauce.

- ☐ 2 T. Dijon mustard
- ☐ 1 t. finely chopped fresh rosemary
- ☐ ½ t. kosher salt
- ☐ ¼ t. cayenne pepper
- ☐ 2 lbs. boneless chicken strips
- ☐ 1 c. grated Parmesan cheese
- ☐ 1 c. panko breadcrumbs
- ☐ Taleggio Cheese Sauce (recipe below)

1. Preheat the oven to 425 degrees. In a medium mixing bowl, combine the mustard, rosemary, salt, and cayenne. Add the chicken strips and toss to coat fully. Set aside.
2. In a medium shallow bowl (I use a rimmed baking sheet), combine the parmesan and panko breadcrumbs. Dip each chicken strip into this mix, covering completely, slightly pressing the coating into the chicken. Set each strip on a plate as you go.
3. Place a wire rack on top of a baking sheet and place the chicken strips on the rack. If you don't have a wire rack, place the strips on a foil-lined baking sheet sprayed with cooking spray. Bake until the strips are golden brown and cooked through, about 20 minutes. Let rest a few minutes before serving.
4. Serve on a platter (feel free to garnish with a smattering of chopped parsley), along with dipping sauces.

Taleggio Cheese Sauce

- ☐ 8 oz. Taleggio cheese, cut into ½-inch cubes (no rind)
- ☐ ½ c. heavy cream
- ☐ Kosher salt

1. Place the cheese cubes in a heat-proof glass bowl.
2. In a small saucepan, heat the cream until it just begins to simmer. Pour over the cheese, and cover with plastic wrap immediately. Let this stand for about 25 minutes.
3. Remove the plastic wrap and use an immersion blender (or a blender) to blend until smooth. Add a pinch of salt. The result should be creamy and smooth.
4. You can keep the sauce refrigerated and reheat it when needed by placing the container in a large bowl and pouring hot water in the bowl, stirring until the sauce is softened and smooth.

Dessert—Hazelnutty Goodness Carrot Cupcakes

Who doesn't love any variation of carrot cake? For this party, I wanted to incorporate my love of carrot cake into a cupcake. This is a recipe I've been making for years, with a bit more oaty-ness due to the addition of oat flour. I also chose chopped hazelnuts as the nut of choice here. (All good carrot cakes have one!) Zest up your cream cheese frosting with some fresh orange zest and top with more chopped nuts (and maybe some sort of Oscars or movie-related cupcake toppers), and you've got a show-stopper on your hands!

Cupcakes
- ¾ c. oat flour
- ¾ c. flour
- ¾ t. baking soda
- 1 t. cinnamon
- ¼ t. nutmeg
- ¼ t. kosher salt
- ¼ c. chopped hazelnuts
- 1/3 c. vegetable oil
- 1/3 c. buttermilk
- 2 eggs
- 1 c. sugar
- 1 t. vanilla
- 1 t. orange zest
- ½ c. crushed pineapple
- 1 c. grated carrots

Cream Cheese Frosting
- 1 8-oz. package cream cheese, room temperature
- 4 T. butter, softened
- 3 c. powdered sugar
- 1 t. vanilla
- 1 T. orange zest
- ½ c. chopped hazelnuts, for garnish

1. Preheat the oven to 350 degrees. Line a 12-muffin tin with cupcake liners.
2. In a medium mixing bowl, whisk together both flours, baking soda, cinnamon, nutmeg, salt, and the hazelnuts. Set aside.
3. In another medium mixing bowl, whisk together the oil, buttermilk, eggs, sugar, vanilla, orange zest, pineapple, and carrots until well mixed. Slowly add the dry mix, and stir until just combined.
4. Distribute the batter evenly in the muffin tins, filling about ¾ full. Bake for 22 minutes, or until golden brown. Let cool completely before frosting.
5. For the frosting, combine the cream cheese and butter in a large mixing bowl. Blend with an electric mixer on low speed until creamy. Add the powdered sugar and mix until well incorporated. Lastly, stir in the vanilla and orange zest. Frost the cupcakes, and sprinkle the chopped hazelnuts on top.

Dessert—Mandarin Cream Delights

I've blogged about this dessert, and it's always been one of my top-requested recipes. It's a lovely fruit concoction with a mix of fresh and canned mandarin oranges. I'm a sucker for old-school, church bake sale–type desserts. Give me a shortbread crust with some type of creamy fruity layer and a whipped cream layer, and I'm the happiest boy at the bake sale. You'll feel like a kid eating this fun and fluffy dessert.

- ☐ 9 T. butter, softened
- ☐ ½ c. sugar
- ☐ 1 t. vanilla extract
- ☐ 1½ c. flour
- ☐ ⅛ t. kosher salt
- ☐ 2 11-oz. cans mandarin oranges
- ☐ 1 24-oz. container sour cream
- ☐ 2 3.4-oz. packages of vanilla instant pudding mix
- ☐ 1 container Cool Whip
- ☐ Fresh mint zest, for garnish
- ☐ Maldon sea salt flakes, for garnish

1. Preheat the oven to 350 degrees. In a medium mixing bowl, Beat the butter, ½ c. sugar, and vanilla with electric beaters until fluffy. Add the flour and salt, and mix well. This will be a buttery, crumbly shortbread dough.

2. Press the dough into a 13 x 9-inch baking dish sprayed with cooking spray. Cook for 13 minutes, or until lightly browned. Let cool completely.

3. Prepare the fruit layer: Drain the mandarin oranges, reserving the juices. In a large mixing bowl, combine ½ c. of reserved mandarin juice (save the rest for later), ¼ c. sugar, sour cream, and pudding mix. Stir in the mandarin oranges. Spoon this mixture over the cooled shortbread crust.

4. Prepare the whipped cream: Combine the Cool Whip with ⅓ cup of the extra mandarin orange juice. Spread over the fruit layer. Let chill for at least 1 hour.

5. Prior to serving, sprinkle the top with mint zest and a sprinkling of sea salt flakes. Cut into squares and serve!

THE PERFECT FESTIVE HOLIDAY DINNER

So, for *A Perfect 10 Party Edition*, here's the menu for my only fully traditional dinner party — you know, where we actually sit around a table, eat family style, and enjoy the holidays. Which holidays you ask? You choose. In my previous cookbook I laid out my decades-in-the-making ultimate Thanksgiving dinner menu. This menu is a different animal — you can use it for any holiday gathering you want. I love cooking for the holidays — it's my chance to get a bit more bougie with the menu items then I usually do — and anytime I get a chance to break out my vintage Tom and Jerry punch bowl and mugs, I'm a happy holiday camper. I include three dessert items for this menu. It's the holidays, so I say make all three!

PARTY GAMES

For a holiday party, I like activities to be played during the dinner, while everyone is seated. I've been known to whip out a flipchart for a rousing mid-dinner round of Pictionary (holiday themed, of course).

Also, for a wild night, you may want to play the never-gets-old and always inappropriate Lap Game. To play, everyone takes a seat. You then read from a list of life events. If someone had the event happen to them, they move to sit on the lap to their left. (There may be a stack of people on the same lap at one point!) The winner is the first person to make it all the way around back to their seat. So fun! Here's a list of life events you can use:

- Have you ever ridden a mule? Eaten frog's legs? Wet your pants? Done the splits?
- Have you hugged someone today?
- Are you not wearing underwear?
- Are you wearing a ring today?
- Were you ever in a high school band?
- Did you fail your first driving test?
- Have you been to Sweden? Run a half marathon?
- Do you have a tattoo?
- Have you ever read *Fifty Shades of Gray*? Rode a mechanical bull? Been to Sea World?
- Have you never watched *Gone with the Wind*?
- Have you ever hitchhiked? Had a crush on a friend's parent? Chipped a tooth?

Add or substitute your own questions to fit the mood of the crowd!

Drinks—Tom and Jerrys and Spicy Holiday Lemonade

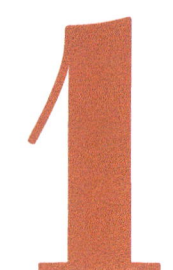

Making a Tom and Jerry cocktail makes me so happy — it reminds me of my mother's holiday parties from the '70s, helped in no small measure by its milky-holiday-spiced smells and flavor. Your younger guests will be thrilled with experiencing a new tradition, and your…well, "more tenured" guests will be beaming with nostalgia. And as a counterbalance, this Spicy Holiday Lemonade is seriously addictive. It screams holiday and is just a fun thing to have a pitcher full of (and help to get the caroling and holiday games in full swing!). Enjoy!

Tom and Jerrys
Each makes 1 pitcher or 4-6 drinks.

- [ ] 2 eggs, separated
- [ ] 1/8 t. cream of tartar
- [ ] 1½ c. + 2 t. dark rum
- [ ] 2/3 c. sugar
- [ ] ¼ t. cinnamon
- [ ] ⅛ t. allspice
- [ ] ⅛ t. ground cloves
- [ ] 4½ c. milk
- [ ] 1½ c. Cognac
- [ ] Nutmeg

1. In a large bowl, whisk together the egg whites and cream of tartar until stiff peaks form.
2. In a separate bowl, whisk the egg yolks, 2 teaspoons rum, sugar, cinnamon, allspice, and cloves until thick and creamy. Slowly fold in the egg whites in small batches. Don't overmix. Cover with plastic wrap and let chill for at least 1 hour in the refrigerator.
3. When ready to serve, heat the milk in a saucepan over medium-low heat. In a mug, add 1 heaping teaspoon of the chilled batter. Stir in 1½ tablespoons each of Cognac and rum. Cover with about 6 ounces of the warmed milk. Stir until frothy and garnish with nutmeg. Repeat for as many as you need. You can also set the batter in a punch bowl and place the mugs around it to let your guests do the mixing.

Spicy Holiday Lemonade

- [ ] 1½ c. vodka
- [ ] ½ c. Pimm's #1
- [ ] 1 c. fresh lemon juice
- [ ] ½ c. fresh lime juice
- [ ] ½ c. honey
- [ ] 2 t. hot sauce
- [ ] 1 t. ground black pepper
- [ ] 1 lemon, thinly sliced
- [ ] 1 lime, thinly sliced
- [ ] 1 c. 7-Up
- [ ] Lime wheels, for garnish

1. In a large container, combine all ingredients except for the lemon, lime, and 7-Up. Vigorously mix or shake and then let chill for at least 1 hour in the refrigerator.
2. In a serving pitcher, add a few cups of ice and the lemon and lime slices. Give the vodka mixture another good shake and then pour into the pitcher. Add the 7-Up and stir well.
3. Serve over ice with a lime wheel garnish.

Appy—French Onion Soup Stuffed Mushrooms

Of course I include a few appy options in all of my *Perfect 10* party menus, and for a holiday dinner you really need to include some version of stuffed mushrooms. There are a million delish options for stuffing the old mushroom cap, but I think this delectable pile of caramelized onions in a French onion soup–inspired broth really does the holiday trick.

- ☐ 2 dozen large cremini mushrooms
- ☐ 2 T. olive oil
- ☐ 3 T. butter
- ☐ 2 onions, thinly sliced
- ☐ 2 t. fresh thyme, finely chopped
- ☐ ¼ c. red wine
- ☐ ½ c. beef broth
- ☐ 1 c. toasted breadcrumbs
- ☐ 1 c. Gruyere cheese, shredded
- ☐ 3 T. Parmesan cheese, grated
- ☐ Chopped parsley, for garnish

1. Prep the mushrooms: Preheat the oven to 425 degrees. Remove the stems from the mushrooms and wipe the inside of the mushroom caps clean with a damp paper towel. In a mixing bowl, toss the mushroom caps with olive oil and a large pinch of kosher salt. Arrange the mushrooms on a baking sheet.

2. Make the topping: In a large skillet over medium heat, melt the butter. Add the onions and thyme and season with a large pinch of salt and a few grinds of fresh black pepper. Cook, stirring occasionally, until the onions are caramelized, about 20 minutes. Add the wine and cook for about 1 minute, letting the wine evaporate. Add the broth and simmer for about 3 minutes.

3. Put it all together: Sprinkle a pinch of breadcrumbs into each mushroom cap. Fill with the onion mixture and then add a pinch of Gruyere and Parmesan cheese on top.

4. Bake for about 16 minutes, or until the mushrooms are tender and the topping is bubbly and golden. Let cool for a few minutes, sprinkle with parsley, and serve!

Appy—Kale Mashed Potatoes

Mashed potatoes are a mainstay of any holiday dinner. I love just throwing in some combination of cheese, garlic, herbs, veggies, Dijon — and they always turn out YUMMY. This recipe puts a bit of an Italian spin on them, and they are fantastic. You can serve them without the gravy, or serve the uber-flavorful Simply Fantastic Gravy on the side. (I make this side all the time and serve it with many dishes.)

- ☐ 5 large russet potatoes, peeled and chopped into 1-in. chunks
- ☐ 4 cloves garlic, minced
- ☐ 2 t. kosher salt
- ☐ 8 T. (1 stick) butter, softened
- ☐ 3 T. olive oil
- ☐ 1 small onion, diced
- ☐ 1 ½ t. fresh ground black pepper
- ☐ 12 oz. kale leaves, chopped
- ☐ 1 c. chicken broth
- ☐ 8 oz. mascarpone cheese, room temperature
- ☐ ¾ c. Parmesan cheese, grated

1. Combine the potatoes, 2 cloves garlic, 1 teaspoon salt, and 2 tablespoons of butter in a large saucepan and cover with cold water. Bring to a boil over medium-high heat. Reduce to a simmer and cook until the potatoes are soft, about 20 minutes. Drain, then return the potatoes to the pan and mash until smooth.

2. Prep the kale: Heat the olive oil in a large skillet over medium-high heat. Add the onion, 1 teaspoon of salt, and ½ teaspoon of pepper. Cook until the onions are well softened, about 5 minutes. Add 2 cloves of garlic and cook for about 1 minute. Add the kale and ½ cup of the broth and cook until the kale is softened, about 10 minutes.

3. Put it all together: To the potatoes, add the kale mixture, mascarpone cheese, ½ cup of broth, 4 tablespoons of butter, Parmesan cheese, 2 teaspoons of salt, and 1 teaspoon of pepper and mix well. Stir, cooking over low heat, until smooth and well mixed. Transfer the potatoes to bowl and garnish with Parmesan cheese. Serve with the Simply Fantastic Gravy on the side.

Simply Fantastic Gravy

- ☐ 2 T. salted butter
- ☐ 1 red onion, thinly sliced
- ☐ ½ t. sugar
- ☐ Kosher salt
- ☐ ½ t. dried oregano
- ☐ 2 T. flour
- ☐ 2 c. beef (or vegetable) broth
- ☐ ¼ c. milk
- ☐ 1 T. nutritional yeast
- ☐ Fresh ground black pepper

1. In a large skillet, melt the butter over medium heat. Add the red onion, sugar, and a pinch of salt. Cook for about 10 minutes, stirring occasionally, until the onions brown and caramelize.

2. Add the oregano and flour and cook, stirring constantly, for about 1 minute. Whisk in the broth and milk, raise the heat to high, and bring to a boil while whisking. Reduce the heat to low, and let simmer for about 5 minutes until slightly thickened, stirring occasionally.

3. Whisk in the nutritional yeast and salt and pepper to taste, and then it's ready to go! You can also store it in the refrigerator and heat when ready to serve.

Side—Fried Brussels with Appley-Fenneley Slaw

I'm sure I'm not the only one who hated Brussels sprouts as a kid — but let's face it, those were old-school, boiled, and pretty gross. Now, of course, Brussels sprouts have a whole new image and taste and are found on pretty much every trendy dinner menu around the globe. They are my family's number-one veggie — we make them pretty much three to four times a week. For this recipe, I'm frying and crisping them up — including what might be my favorite culinary garnish, fried Brussels sprouts leaves! Add an apple-fennel slaw and mustardy goodness in a vinaigrette, and your holiday guests will be reveling in HO HO HOme-cooked holiday goodness!

- ☐ ⅔ c. crème fraiche
- ☐ ⅓ c. whole grain mustard
- ☐ 2 T. apple cider vinegar
- ☐ 1 T. honey
- ☐ Fresh ground black pepper
- ☐ 2 lbs. Brussels sprouts, halved
- ☐ Canola oil, for frying
- ☐ 1 green apple, cut into very thin stick-like slices
- ☐ 1 fennel bulb, cut into very thin stick-like slices
- ☐ Kosher salt

1. Prepare the dressing: In a small mixing bowl, whisk the crème fraiche, mustard, vinegar, and honey. Season with salt and fresh ground black pepper. Set aside.

2. Pluck the outer leaves from the Brussels sprouts, enough to yield about 1 ½ cups. Set aside.

3. Pour about 2 inches of canola oil into a large frying pan. Heat over medium-high heat. Add the Brussels sprouts in small batches — they should begin to sizzle immediately. Cook until golden brown and crispy, about 5 minutes per batch. Remove with a slotted spoon and place on a cooling rack. Sprinkle with salt. Repeat with all of the sprouts.

4. Repeat Step 3 with the plucked Brussels sprouts leaves, cooking until browned and crispy. Transfer the leaves to a plate lined with paper towels and immediately sprinkle with salt.

5. Spread the Brussels sprouts on a platter. Drizzle half of the dressing over the top. Season with salt and pepper.

6. In a small mixing bowl, toss the apple and fennel slices with the remaining dressing and scatter over the top of the sprouts. Sprinkle the fried leaves on top.

Side—Spicy Creamy Cheesy Corn

It's hard to top the Not Your Grandmother's Creamed Corn recipe in *A Perfect 10* (in the "Thanksgiving" chapter), but this recipe just might do it. It is packed with so much unique flavor, and will be so unlike any creamed corn dish your guests will have ever experienced, that they will all be clamoring for more. What's the special ingredient? Two of my favorite products: Taleggio cheese (hello, Taleggio Cheese Sauce on page 127) and the amazing doenjang Korean soybean paste. Take a chance, make it, and I promise it will become a dinner party mainstay at your house!

- ☐ 6 slices bacon, cut into small pieces
- ☐ ¾ c. panko breadcrumbs
- ☐ ¼ t. kosher salt
- ☐ ¼ c. olive oil
- ☐ 3 ½ c. sweet yellow (or white) corn kernels
- ☐ ¾ c. milk
- ☐ 1 ½ oz. Taleggio cheese, grated
- ☐ 2 T. doenjang
- ☐ 1 t. soy sauce
- ☐ ½ c. mozzarella cheese, grated
- ☐ 1 green onion, sliced

1. Cook the bacon in a large saucepan over medium heat until crispy. Transfer the bacon to a plate lined with paper towels. Add the panko breadcrumbs and salt to the pan and cook until golden brown, about 3 minutes. Transfer to a small mixing bowl and add about ⅓ of the cooked bacon. Toss and set aside.

2. In a separate large saucepan, heat 2 tablespoons of the olive oil over medium heat. Add 1 ½ cups of the corn kernels. Cook for about 3 minutes. Add the milk and bring to a simmer, then reduce the heat to low and let simmer, stirring occasionally, until the liquid has reduced significantly, about 20 minutes.

3. In a blender, combine the Taleggio cheese, doenjang, soy sauce, and the corn-milk mixture, blending until smooth.

4. In a large Dutch oven or heavy saucepan, heat the remaining 2 tablespoons of olive oil. Add the remaining cooked bacon and remaining 2 cups of corn kernels, and cook, stirring, for about 3 minutes. Add the Taleggio mixture and stir until well mixed. Stir in the mozzarella cheese until melted. Season with salt.

5. Transfer to a serving bowl, top with the panko-bacon mix and chopped green onion, and serve!

Main—Tim's Turkey Milanese with Arugula Salad

Any entrée with the label "Milanese" is a winner in my book. You can make this recipe with chicken, pork, tofu — or whatever is your protein pleasure. But I think pounded turkey breasts are the way to go, and turkey already says HOLIDAY DINNER loud and clear. But it's the paste you make from Dijon, lemon zest, and garlic that really elevates this dish and provides its Milanese Medal of Honor. Of course, you have to top it with an arugula salad dressed with this simple Italian vinaigrette that you can literally drizzle over anything. Happy holidays!

The Turkey
- ☐ 2 lbs. boneless turkey breasts
- ☐ ¾ c. flour
- ☐ 1 ¾ c. panko breadcrumbs (or regular Italian breadcrumbs)
- ☐ 2 egg whites
- ☐ 3 T. Dijon mustard
- ☐ 3 garlic cloves, minced
- ☐ 2 t. dried oregano
- ☐ Zest of 1 lemon
- ☐ Vegetable oil, for frying

1. Place the turkey breasts on a cutting board and cover them with a sheet of plastic wrap. Pound the breasts into thin pieces, about ¼-inch thick. Season both sides with salt and pepper.

2. Take 3 plates; to one plate add the flour. To another add the breadcrumbs. Then, in a small mixing bowl, combine the egg whites, Dijon, garlic, oregano, and lemon zest. Add this mix to the third plate.

3. Dredge each turkey cutlet in the flour. Cover it with the egg mixture, and then roll it in the breadcrumbs. Do this for all of the cutlets. Place them on a platter and chill for 1 hour.

4. When ready to cook the cutlets, add about ½-inch of oil to a large frying pan and heat over medium-high heat. When the cutlet sizzles when you add it, it's ready. Cook for 4 minutes on one side, then flip and cook for about 3 minutes on the other. They should be a golden brown on both sides. Let the cutlets drain on a paper towel-lined plate, and season both sides with salt and pepper. Serve on a platter with the salad piled on top and the rest of the salad dressing on the side to drizzle on the turkey, if desired.

The Salad

- Juice of 1 large lemon
- 2 T. coarse Dijon mustard
- 1 T. smooth Dijon mustard
- ¼ c. olive oil
- 5 oz. arugula
- 1 small fennel bulb, sliced as thin as you can go

1. In a small bowl, whisk together the lemon juice and mustards. Slowly whisk in the olive oil. Set aside.
2. In a large bowl, pour in about ¾ of the dressing. Add the arugula and sliced fennel and toss well.

Main—Perfect Pork Loin with Chunky Applesauce

A roasted pork loin makes the perfect holiday dinner main course. It's super tender and flavorful, and easy to prepare as well. Pair with a homemade chunky applesauce, and you have a real stunner.

- ¾ c. Dijon mustard
- Juice and zest of 1 lemon
- 2 T. fresh thyme
- 2 T. butter, softened
- 4 T. olive oil
- 1 boneless pork loin roast (3–4 lbs.)
- 2 large onions, sliced
- 8 c. apple cider
- 1 bundle fresh thyme, tied with string
- 3 bay leaves

1. Preheat the oven to 450 degrees. In a medium mixing bowl, whisk together the Dijon, lemon juice and zest, thyme, and butter. Set aside.

2. Season the pork loin with salt and pepper. In a large skillet (cast iron if you have it), heat 2 tablespoons of the olive oil. Place the pork loin in the pan and let it brown on all sides, about 2 minutes per side. When it is nicely browned, you're ready for the next step.

3. In a medium bowl, toss the onions with the remaining 2 tablespoons of olive oil, 5 cups of the cider, the thyme bundle, and the bay leaves. Pour this mixture around the bottom of a roasting pan.

4. Slather the Dijon mixture over the pork loin, place the pork on top of the onions, and roast in the oven for about 40 minutes, or until a nice brown crust has developed on the pork. Add more cider to the pan if needed.

5. Cook until the pork reaches a temperature of 136 degrees. Remove from the oven and let it rest for at least 15 minutes. Reserve 2 cups of cider from the pan and set aside. While the pork is resting, make the applesauce.

6. When ready to serve, slice the pork into thin slices. Place on a platter, scatter the braised onions over the top, and serve with the applesauce on the side.

Chunky Applesauce

- 3 T. butter
- 4 green apples, peeled and cut into small chunks
- 2 cups of reserved cider from the pork loin
- ¼ c. apple cider
- 1 t. cinnamon
- ¼ c. heavy cream
- ½ c. pecans, toasted and chopped

1. In a large saucepan, melt the butter. Add the apples and cook over medium-low heat until they start to soften. Add the reserved cider, apple cider, and cinnamon, and cook until most of the cider has evaporated and the apples are soft.
2. Add the heavy cream and pecans, and cook until the cream reduces by half. You should now have a chunky, savory applesauce.

Dessert—Dreamy Lemon Ginger Cake

This little gem of a cake makes for a perfect end to your holiday meal. Loaded with ginger, molasses, and lemon, it's so festive and delicious. To ramp up the holiday quotient, I like to add some candied cranberries — this is a topping you can use for many of your holiday desserts. Go ho ho for it!

The Cake
- ☐ 8 T. (1 stick) butter, softened
- ☐ ½ c. brown sugar
- ☐ 2 eggs
- ☐ ½ c. molasses
- ☐ 2 t. lemon zest
- ☐ 1½ c. flour
- ☐ 2 t. ground ginger
- ☐ ½ t. baking soda
- ☐ ½ t. salt
- ☐ ½ c. milk
- ☐ 1/3 c. crystallized ginger, chopped
- ☐ 1½ c. heavy cream
- ☐ ¼ c. powdered sugar
- ☐ 2 T. sugar
- ☐ 2 T. crème fraiche
- ☐ 1 t. vanilla extract

1. Preheat the oven to 350 degrees. Grease one 8-inch round cake pan, line with parchment paper, and then grease the top of the parchment paper.
2. In a standing mixer, cream the butter and brown sugar for about 4 minutes, or until fluffy. Add the eggs, molasses, and lemon zest and mix well.
3. In a separate bowl, whisk together the flour, ginger, baking soda, and salt. Slowly mix this into the wet ingredients. Once well combined, add the milk and mix until smooth. Gently fold in the crystallized ginger. Pour into the cake pan and bake for about 30 minutes, or until a toothpick in the center comes out clean. Let cool.
4. Make the whipped cream topping: Combine the heavy cream, powdered sugar, sugar, crème fraiche, and vanilla in a mixing bowl and whip until soft peaks form. Decorate the cake with this topping, and then sprinkle the sugared cranberries and some crystalized ginger bits over the top.

Sugared Cranberries
- ☐ ½ c. water
- ☐ ¾ c. sugar
- ☐ 1 c. cranberries
- ☐ 1 t. cardamom

1. In a small saucepan, whisk the water and ½ cup of the sugar to combine. Bring to a simmer and whisk until the sugar is dissolved. Remove from heat and stir in the cranberries so that they are coated evenly with the sugar syrup. Cover and let steep for at least 10 minutes.
2. Strain the cranberries. Mix the remaining ¼ c. sugar with the cardamom. Toss in the cranberries, covering them completely with the sugar mixture.

Dessert—Blueberry Oatmeal Crisp with No-Churn Ice Cream

This bubbly and gooey fruit crisp is the perfect accompaniment to any holiday dinner menu — and the lemon-infused blueberry version is always a hit. For the topping, you can use any chopped nut, but I think hazelnuts add the best rich and nutty flavor. And for the ice cream, I make this no-churn variety constantly, adding whatever "extra" flavor enhancements I desire — from peanut butter to fruit preserves to pretzels to cookie crumbles to chocolate chips. It's so easy and requires no special equipment.

Blueberry Filling
- ☐ 6 c. blueberries
- ☐ ½ c. sugar
- ☐ 3 T. flour
- ☐ 2 T. lemon juice
- ☐ ½ t. salt

Oat Topping
- ☐ ¾ c. brown sugar
- ☐ ¾ c. flour
- ☐ ½ c. old-fashioned oats
- ☐ ½ c. chopped hazelnuts
- ☐ Zest of 1 lemon
- ☐ ¼ t. cinnamon
- ☐ ½ t. salt
- ☐ 6 T. cold butter, cut into small slices

1. Preheat the oven to 375 degrees. Generously grease a 2-quart baking dish.
2. Make the blueberry filling: In a medium bowl, stir together the filling ingredients. Once mixed well, pour into the prepared baking dish.
3. Make the oat topping: Combine all ingredients but the butter, and mix well. Using your fingers, work in the butter slices, squishing everything together until it becomes a buttery, crumbly mixture. Sprinkle this over the blueberry filling.
4. Bake until the topping is golden brown and the berry mix is nice and bubbly. Serve with ice cream.

No-Churn Ice Cream
- ☐ 2 c. heavy cream
- ☐ 1 14-oz. can sweetened condensed milk
- ☐ 1 t. vanilla
- ☐ Pinch of salt
- ☐ Optional add-ins: ½ c. granola, oatmeal cookie chunks, blueberry jam, almond butter, peanut butter

1. In a stand mixer, whip the heavy cream until stiff peaks form, about 5 minutes.

2. In a large bowl, whisk together the milk, vanilla, salt, and the optional add-in (for the blueberry oatmeal crisp, I like to add broken oatmeal cookies).

3. Carefully fold the whipped cream into the milk mixture (about a scoop at a time). Don't overmix it.

4. Transfer to a loaf pan, cover with plastic wrap, and let freeze at least 4 hours.

Dessert—Aunt Pat's Chocolate Espresso Cream "Pie"

To complete my trifecta of classic holiday dinner desserts, here's a cream pie! This recipe hails from my beloved Aunt Pat, whose recipes I've hijacked and featured in my cookbooks and blogs quite often. This is really a three-layer pie with a nutty, buttery crust. The addition of espresso powder to the whipped cream is a great enhancement. Thanks, Aunt Pat, at whose holiday dinner parties I've been a lucky guest my entire life. Yum!

- ☐ 1 c. flour
- ☐ ½ c. chopped pecans
- ☐ ½ c. butter
- ☐ 2 T. powdered sugar
- ☐ Kosher salt
- ☐ 1 c. whipped topping
- ☐ 1 c. powdered sugar
- ☐ 8 oz. cream cheese, softened
- ☐ 2 small packages instant chocolate pudding
- ☐ 3 c. milk
- ☐ 3 t. vanilla
- ☐ 1 c. mini chocolate chips (and extra for garnish)
- ☐ 1 ⅓ c. heavy cream
- ☐ 1 t. espresso powder
- ☐ 3 T. sugar
- ☐ Chocolate shavings, for garnish

1. Make the crust: Preheat the oven to 350 degrees. Mix together the flour, nuts, butter, powdered sugar, and a pinch of salt. (Using your hands is the best way.) Pat this buttery dough into a glass pie pan. Bake for about 20 to 25 minutes, or until lightly browned. Let cool completely.

2. Prepare the filling: In a mixing bowl, combine the whipped topping, powdered sugar, and cream cheese. Beat until fluffy. Spread over the cooled pie crust.

3. In a separate mixing bowl, mix together the pudding mixes, milk, and 1 teaspoon of vanilla extract, and beat until thickened. Stir in the chocolate chips. Spread over the cream cheese layer.

4. For the final layer — espresso whipped cream — beat the heavy cream in a separate bowl until soft peaks form. Add the espresso powder, sugar, and remaining 2 teaspoons of vanilla, and continue mixing until you see stiff peaks. This layer goes on top of the chocolate layer.

5. Garnish with chocolate shavings and extra chocolate chips. Keep in the refrigerator until ready to serve. Mmm!

Index

A

Alluring Arugula Pear Salad, 119
almond butter
   Blueberry Almond Butter
      Smoothies, 9
   Mouthwatering Chicken
      Mole Tostadas, 121
almond flour
   Lovely and Lemony Olive
      Oil Cake, 107
Almondy Caesar Salad, 53
Antipasto Salad, 75
Aperol
   Beer-Perol Surprises, 25
appetizers
   Baked Bacon Crackers, 31
   Cheesy Olive Puffs, 93
   Cocktail Meatballs with
      Grape Jelly, 27
   Cubano Tots! 49
   French Onion Soup Stuffed
      Mushrooms, 137
   Greek Pita Walking Taco
      Snack Bags, 117
   Kale Mashed Potatoes, 138–139
   Mini Sausage Corn Pups, 29
   Ooey Gooey Hot Curry
      Cambozola Dip, 5
   Party Popovers, 51
   Pimento Dip, 71
   Rosemary Spiced Candied Bacon, 7
   Zestylicious Mexi Layered Dip, 32
apple cider
   Perfect Pork Loin with Chunky
      Applesauce, 146–147
apples
   Fried Brussels with Appley-
      Fenneley Slaw, 141
   Grilled Turkey-Apple Burgers, 83
   Ooey Gooey Hot Curry
      Cambozola Dip, 5
   Perfect Pork Loin with Chunky
      Applesauce, 146–147
   Princess Leia Cinnamon
      Roll Apple Pie, 21
   Sublime Sangria (Boozy
      and Not Boozy), 91
artichoke hearts
   Antipasto Salad, 75
arugula
   Alluring Arugula Pear Salad, 119
   Antipasto Salad, 75
   Grilled Turkey-Apple Burgers, 83

Tim's Turkey Milanese with
   Arugula Salad, 144–145
Asiago cheese
   Party Popovers, 51
Aunt Pat's Chocolate Espresso
   Cream "Pie," 153
avocados
   Grilled Chicken Cobb Salad, 81
   Mulli Guacamole, 33
   The Quick(est) and Easy(iest)
      Amazing Layered Dip, 115

B

bacon
   Baked Bacon Crackers, 31
   BBQ Beans with Turkey Bacon, 79
   Breakfast-y Pasta Salad, 11
   Grilled Chicken Cobb Salad, 81
   Mac and Cheese Station, 35
   Pineapple Bacon Upside-
      Down Cake, 63
   Rosemary Spiced Candied Bacon, 7
   Spicy Creamy Cheesy Corn, 143
Baked Bacon Crackers, 31
Balloon Popping, 89
Basic Vinaigrette, 119
basil
   Antipasto Salad, 75
   Basil Oil, 58
   Cheesy Egg and Polenta Casserole, 13
   Spicy Veggie Lasagna, 58–59
   Sublime Sangria (Boozy
      and Not Boozy), 91
   Tiny Thai Basil Beef Bowls, 105
BBQ Beans with Turkey Bacon, 79
BBQ Sauce, Da Bomb, 122, 123
beans
   BBQ Beans with Turkey Bacon, 79
   Tantalizing Texas-Style Bean Soup, 125
   Zestylicious Mexi Layered Dip, 32

beef
   Blackened Flank Steak
      and Corny Salsa, 61
   Can't-Eat-Just-One
      Western Sliders, 122
   Cocktail Meatballs with Grape Jelly, 27
   Greek Pita Walking Taco
      Snack Bags, 117
   Loco Moco Nachos, 36
   Tiny Thai Basil Beef Bowls, 105
beer
   Beer-Perol Surprises, 25
   Mulligan Micheladas, 47
   Orange Shandys, 69
berries
   Watermelon-Mint Salad, 73
berry liqueur
   Sublime Sangria (Boozy
      and Not Boozy), 91
BEST Birthday Cake with
   No-Churn Ice Cream, The, 65
Bingo, 45, 111
black beans
   Tantalizing Texas-Style Bean Soup, 125
blackberries
   Cup o' Grapes Fruit Salad, 99
   Sublime Sangria (Boozy
      and Not Boozy), 91
   Watermelon-Mint Salad, 73
Blackened Flank Steak and
   Corny Salsa, 61
blue cheese
   Grilled Chicken Cobb Salad, 81
blueberries
   Blueberry Almond Butter Smoothies, 9
   Blueberry Oatmeal Crisp with
      No-Churn Ice Cream, 150–151
   Watermelon-Mint Salad, 73
Boozy Sangria, 91
bread
   Almondy Caesar Salad, 53

Pickle-Craving Finger Sandwiches, 101
Breakfast-y Pasta Salad, 11
Brownies, Irish Cream
    Delectable Chocolate, 41
Brussels with Appley-Fenneley
    Slaw, Fried, 141
buttermilk
    Chocolate Cold Brew Pistachio
        Cake Cups, 85
    Grilled Chicken Cobb Salad, 81
    Hazelnutty Goodness
        Carrot Cupcakes, 129
    Mini Sausage Corn Pups, 29
    Pineapple Bacon Upside-
        Down Cake, 63

C

cakes
    Chocolaty Goodness Coffee Cake, 19
    Dreamy Lemon Ginger Cake, 149
    Hazelnutty Goodness
        Carrot Cupcakes, 129
    Lovely and Lemony Olive Oil Cake, 107
Cambozola Dip, Ooey Gooey Hot Curry, 5
cannellini beans
    BBQ Beans with Turkey Bacon, 79
Can't-Eat-Just-One Western Sliders, 122
capers
    Spicy Veggie Lasagna, 58–59
    Tasty Turkey Picadillo Cups, 103
carrots
    Hazelnutty Goodness
        Carrot Cupcakes, 129
    Mouthwatering Chicken
        Mole Tostadas, 121
Chambord
    Sublime Sangria (Boozy
        and Not Boozy), 91
Champagne
    Lemon Chiffon Punch, 47

charades, 45
cheddar cheese
    Can't-Eat-Just-One
        Western Sliders, 122
    Cheesy Olive Puffs, 93
    Mac and Cheese Station, 35
    Pickle-Craving Finger Sandwiches, 101
    Pimento Dip, 71
    Tantalizing Texas-Style Bean Soup, 125
cheese. see *individual cheese types*
Cheesy Olive Puffs, 93
cherries
    Partridges in Pear Trees, 3
    Pineapple Bacon Upside-
        Down Cake, 63
chicken
    Delectable Curry Chicken Salad, 95
    Grilled Chicken Cobb Salad, 81
    Mini-Chicken and Waffles, 39
    Mouthwatering Chicken
        Mole Tostadas, 121
    Primo Parmesan-Crusted
        Chicken Strips, 127
chickpeas. see garbanzo beans
chili sauce
    Cocktail Meatballs with Grape Jelly, 27
chocolate
    Aunt Pat's Chocolate Espresso
        Cream "Pie," 153
    Chocolate Cold Brew Pistachio
        Cake Cups, 85
    Chocolaty Goodness Coffee Cake, 19
    Irish Cream Delectable
        Chocolate Brownies, 41
chocolate, white
    The BEST Birthday Cake with
        No-Churn Ice Cream, 65
chorizo
    Chorizo Hash, 17
    The Quick(est) and Easy(iest)
        Amazing Layered Dip, 115

see also sausage
Chunky Applesauce, 146–147
cilantro
   Blackened Flank Steak
      and Corny Salsa, 61
   Delectable Curry Chicken Salad, 95
   Hawaiian Slaw, 37
   Mouthwatering Chicken
      Mole Tostadas, 121
   Mulli Guacamole, 33
   The Quick(est) and Easy(iest)
      Amazing Layered Dip, 115
   Tantalizing Texas-Style Bean Soup, 125
   Your New Favorite Coconut-
      Cilantro Rice, 97
   Zestylicious Mexi Layered Dip, 32
Cocktail Meatballs with Grape Jelly, 27
cocoa powder
   The BEST Birthday Cake with
      No-Churn Ice Cream, 65
   Chocolate Cold Brew Pistachio
      Cake Cups, 85
   Mouthwatering Chicken
      Mole Tostadas, 121
Coconut-Cilantro Rice, Your
   New Favorite, 97
coffee/espresso
   Aunt Pat's Chocolate Espresso
      Cream "Pie," 153
   Chocolate Cold Brew Pistachio
      Cake Cups, 85
cognac
   Tom and Jerrys, 134
coleslaw mix
   Hawaiian Slaw, 37
Cookies, Honey-Butter Shortbread, 43
corn
   Blackened Flank Steak
      and Corny Salsa, 61
   Spicy Creamy Cheesy Corn, 143
   Zestylicious Mexi Layered Dip, 32

corn flakes
   Mini-Chicken and Waffles, 39
cornmeal
   Mini Sausage Corn Pups, 29
Cotija cheese
   Zestylicious Mexi Layered Dip, 32
crackers
   Baked Bacon Crackers, 31
   Cocktail Meatballs with Grape Jelly, 27
   Delectable Curry Chicken Salad, 95
   Lemon-Lime Chiffon Pie, Oh My! 109
cranberries
   Dreamy Lemon Ginger Cake, 149
   Partridge in a Pear Trees, 3
cranberries, dried
   Ooey Gooey Hot Curry
      Cambozola Dip, 5
cranberry juice
   Sublime Sangria (Boozy
      and Not Boozy), 91
cream cheese
   Aunt Pat's Chocolate Espresso
      Cream "Pie," 153
   Cream Cheese Frosting, 129
   Cup o' Grapes Fruit Salad, 99
   Hazelnutty Goodness
      Carrot Cupcakes, 129
   Irish Cream Delectable
      Chocolate Brownies, 41
   Pimento Dip, 71
   Pretzel Salad Cups, 87
crema
   The Quick(est) and Easy(iest)
      Amazing Layered Dip, 115
crème fraiche
   Dreamy Lemon Ginger Cake, 149
   Fried Brussels with Appley-
      Fenneley Slaw, 141
Cubano Tots! 49
cucumbers
   Breakfast-y Pasta Salad, 11

Delectable Curry Chicken Salad, 95
Greek Pita Walking Taco Snack Bags, 117
Hawaiian Macaroni Salad, 77
Pimm's Cups, 113
Tiny Thai Basil Beef Bowls, 105
Cup o' Grapes Fruit Salad, 99

D

Da Bomb BBQ Sauce, 122, 123
Delectable Curry Chicken Salad, 95
desserts
    Aunt Pat's Chocolate Espresso Cream "Pie," 153
    The BEST Birthday Cake with No-Churn Ice Cream, 65
    Blueberry Oatmeal Crisp with No-Churn Ice Cream, 150–151
    Chocolate Cold Brew Pistachio Cake Cups, 85
    Chocolaty Goodness Coffee Cake, 19
    Dreamy Lemon Ginger Cake, 149
    Hazelnutty Goodness Carrot Cupcakes, 129
    Honey-Butter Shortbread Cookies, 43
    Irish Cream Delectable Chocolate Brownies, 41
    Lemon-Lime Chiffon Pie, Oh My! 109
    Lovely and Lemony Olive Oil Cake, 107
    Mandarin Cream Delights, 131
    Pineapple Bacon Upside-Down Cake, 63
    Pretzel Salad Cups, 87
    Princess Leia Cinnamon Roll Apple Pie, 21
Dijon mustard
    Almondy Caesar Salad, 53
    BBQ Beans with Turkey Bacon, 79
    Da Bomb BBQ Sauce, 123
    Grilled Chicken Cobb Salad, 81
    Mac and Cheese Station, 35
    Mini Sausage Corn Pups, 29
    Perfect Pork Loin with Chunky Applesauce, 146–147
    Pickle-Craving Finger Sandwiches, 101
    Primo Parmesan-Crusted Chicken Strips, 127
    Tim's Turkey Milanese with Arugula Salad, 144–145
doenjang
    Spicy Creamy Cheesy Corn, 143
Dreamy Lemon Ginger Cake, 149
drinking games, 23
drinks
    Beer-Perol Surprises, 25
    Blueberry Almond Butter Smoothies, 9
    Fizzy Fun Pink Lemonade, 3
    Hemingway Daiquiris, 69
    Lemon Chiffon Punch, 47
    Mulligan Micheladas, 47
    Orange Shandys, 69
    Partridges in Pear Trees, 3
    Pimm's Cups, 113
    Strawberry Bubblies, 113
    Sublime Sangria (Boozy and Not Boozy), 91
    Tom and Jerrys, 134
    Vodka Giddyups, 25

E

eggs
    Breakfast-y Pasta Salad, 11
    Cheesy Egg and Polenta Casserole, 13
    Fluffy Green Onion Cloud Eggs, 15
    Grilled Chicken Cobb Salad, 81
    Hawaiian Macaroni Salad, 77
    Hawaiian Slaw, 37
    Tom and Jerrys, 134
Espresso Cream "Pie," Aunt Pat's Chocolate, 153

F

Farkle, 45, 67
fennel bulb
  Fried Brussels with Appley-Fenneley Slaw, 141
  Tim's Turkey Milanese with Arugula Salad, 144–145
feta cheese
  Greek Pita Walking Taco Snack Bags, 117
Fibbage, 45
Fizzy Fun Pink Lemonade, 3
Flank Steak and Corny Salsa, Blackened, 61
Fluffy Green Onion Cloud Eggs, 15
Framboise
  Sublime Sangria (Boozy and Not Boozy), 91
French Onion Soup Stuffed Mushrooms, 137
Fried Brussels with Appley-Fenneley Slaw, 141
Fuzzy Duck, 23

G

games
  for awards show parties, 111
  for baby showers, 89
  for birthday parties, 45
  for brunch, 1
  for happy hour, 23
  for holidays, 133
  for pool parties, 67
garbanzo beans
  Yummus! Yogurt Dip, 55
garlic
  BBQ Beans with Turkey Bacon, 79
  Cheesy Olive Puffs, 93
  Delectable Curry Chicken Salad, 95
  Grilled Chicken Cobb Salad, 81
  Kale Mashed Potatoes, 138–139
  Mac and Cheese Station, 35
  Pimento Dip, 71
  Spicy Veggie Lasagna, 58–59
  Tasty Turkey Picadillo Cups, 103
  Tim's Turkey Milanese with Arugula Salad, 144–145
  Tiny Thai Basil Beef Bowls, 105
gin
  Fizzy Fun Pink Lemonade, 3
ginger, crystallized
  Dreamy Lemon Ginger Cake, 149
ginger ale
  Pimm's Cups, 113
ginger beer
  Pimm's Cups, 113
gorgonzola crumbles
  Alluring Arugula Pear Salad, 119
Grape Jelly, Cocktail Meatballs with, 27
grapefruit bitters
  Beer-Perol Surprises, 25
grapefruit juice
  Beer-Perol Surprises, 25
  Hemingway Daiquiris, 69
Grapes Fruit Salad, Cup o,' 99
Great Northern beans
  BBQ Beans with Turkey Bacon, 79
Greek Pita Walking Taco Snack Bags, 117
Grilled Chicken Cobb Salad, 81
Grilled Turkey Apple Burgers, 83
Gruyere cheese
  French Onion Soup Stuffed Mushrooms, 137
  Mac and Cheese Station, 35
guacamole
  Mulli Guacamole, 33
  Zestylicious Mexi Layered Dip, 32

H

ham

Cubano Tots! 49
Hawaiian Macaroni Salad, 77
Party Popovers, 51
Hawaiian Macaroni Salad, 77
Hawaiian Slaw, 36, 37
hazelnuts
    Blueberry Oatmeal Crisp with
        No-Churn Ice Cream, 150–151
    Hazelnutty Goodness
        Carrot Cupcakes, 129
Hemingway Daiquiris, 69
honey
    Beer-Perol Surprises, 25
    Cup o' Grapes Fruit Salad, 99
    Honey-Butter Shortbread Cookies, 43
    Spicy Holiday Lemonade, 134–135
hummus
    Greek Pita Walking Taco Snack Bags, 117
    The Quick(est) and Easy(iest)
        Amazing Layered Dip, 115

I

Ice Cream, Blueberry Oatmeal
    Crisp with No-Churn, 150–151
Irish Cream Delectable
    Chocolate Brownies, 41

J

jalapenos
    Blackened Flank Steak
        and Corny Salsa, 61
    Tiny Thai Basil Beef Bowls, 105
    Zestylicious Mexi Layered Dip, 32
Jello
    Pretzel Salad Cups, 87

K

Kale Mashed Potatoes, 138–139

L

lager beer
    Mulligan Micheladas, 47
Lap Game, 133
Lemon Chiffon Punch, 47
lemonade
    Fizzy Fun Pink Lemonade, 3
    Pimm's Cups, 113
    Spicy Holiday Lemonade, 134–135
Lemon-Lime Chiffon Pie, Oh My! 109
lemon-lime soda
    Sublime Sangria (Boozy
        and Not Boozy), 91
lemons/lemon juice
    Almondy Caesar Salad, 53
    Blueberry Oatmeal Crisp with
        No-Churn Ice Cream, 150–151
    Chocolate Cold Brew Pistachio
        Cake Cups, 85
    Grilled Turkey-Apple Burgers, 83
    Lemon Chiffon Punch, 47
    Lemon-Lime Chiffon Pie, Oh My! 109
    Lemony Fettucine Alfredo, 57
    Lovely and Lemony Olive Oil Cake, 107
    Perfect Pork Loin with Chunky
        Applesauce, 146–147
    Pimm's Cups, 113
    Spicy Holiday Lemonade, 134–135
    Tim's Turkey Milanese with
        Arugula Salad, 144–145
    Vodka Giddyups, 25
    Watermelon-Mint Salad, 73
lettuce
    Almondy Caesar Salad, 53
    Grilled Chicken Cobb Salad, 81
limes/lime juice
    Blackened Flank Steak
        and Corny Salsa, 61
    Delectable Curry Chicken Salad, 95
    Hemingway Daiquiris, 69

Lemon-Lime Chiffon Pie, Oh My! 109
Mulli Guacamole, 33
Mulligan Micheladas, 47
The Quick(est) and Easy(iest)
   Amazing Layered Dip, 115
Spicy Holiday Lemonade, 134–135
Tiny Thai Basil Beef Bowls, 105
Your New Favorite Coconut-
   Cilantro Rice, 97
Zestylicious Mexi Layered Dip, 32
line dancing, 23
Loco Moco Nachos, 36
Lovely and Lemony Olive Oil Cake, 107

M

Mac and Cheese Station, 35
main dishes
   Blackened Flank Steak
     and Corny Salsa, 61
   Can't-Eat-Just-One
     Western Sliders, 122
   Cheesy Egg and Polenta Casserole, 13
   Chorizo Hash, 17
   Fluffy Green Onion Cloud Eggs, 15
   Grilled Chicken Cobb Salad, 81
   Grilled Turkey-Apple Burgers, 83
   Lemony Fettucine Alfredo, 57
   Loco Moco Nachos, 36
   Mac and Cheese Station, 35
   Mini-Chicken and Waffles, 39
   Mouthwatering Chicken
     Mole Tostadas, 121
   Perfect Pork Loin with Chunky
     Applesauce, 146–147
   Pickle-Craving Finger Sandwiches, 101
   Primo Parmesan-Crusted
     Chicken Strips, 127
   Spicy Veggie Lasagna, 58–59
   Tantalizing Texas-Style Bean Soup, 125
Tasty Turkey Picadillo Cups, 103
Tim's Turkey Milanese with
   Arugula Salad, 144–145
Tiny Thai Basil Beef Bowls, 105
Mandarin Cream Delights, 131
mango chutney
   Grilled Turkey-Apple Burgers, 83
maple syrup
   BBQ Beans with Turkey Bacon, 79
   Blueberry Almond Butter Smoothies, 9
   Mini-Chicken and Waffles, 39
maraschino cherries
   Pineapple Bacon Upside-
     Down Cake, 63
maraschino liqueur
   Hemingway Daiquiris, 69
Marco Polo, 67
mascarpone cheese
   Chocolate Cold Brew Pistachio
     Cake Cups, 85
   Kale Mashed Potatoes, 138–139
Mini Sausage Corn Pups, 29
Mini-Chicken and Waffles, 39
mint
   Cup o' Grapes Fruit Salad, 99
   Pimm's Cups, 113
   Watermelon-Mint Salad, 73
Mocktail Sangria, 91
molasses
   Dreamy Lemon Ginger Cake, 149
Mole Tostadas, Mouthwatering
   Chicken, 121
Mouthwatering Chicken
   Mole Tostadas, 121
mozzarella cheese
   Antipasto Salad, 75
   Cheesy Egg and Polenta Casserole, 13
   Spicy Creamy Cheesy Corn, 143
   Spicy Veggie Lasagna, 58–59
Mulli Guacamole, 32, 33
Mulligan Micheladas, 47

mushrooms
    Antipasto Salad, 75
    French Onion Soup Stuffed
        Mushrooms, 137
    Loco Moco Nachos, 36
    Spicy Veggie Lasagna, 58–59
music playlists, 1

N

Nachos, Loco Moco, 36
"Name that Baby Tune," 89
nutritional yeast
    Simply Fantastic Gravy, 138–139
nuts. *see individual nut types*

O

oat flour
    Hazelnutty Goodness
        Carrot Cupcakes, 129
Oatmeal Crisp with No-Churn Ice
    Cream, Blueberry, 150–151
Olive Oil Cake, Lovely and Lemony, 107
olives
    Antipasto Salad, 75
    Cheesy Olive Puffs, 93
    Greek Pita Walking Taco Snack Bags, 117
    Mac and Cheese Station, 35
    Spicy Veggie Lasagna, 58–59
    Tasty Turkey Picadillo Cups, 103
Onesie Decorating, 89
onions
    BBQ Beans with Turkey Bacon, 79
    Chorizo Hash, 17
    Cocktail Meatballs with Grape Jelly, 27
    French Onion Soup Stuffed
        Mushrooms, 137
    Grilled Chicken Cobb Salad, 81
    Hawaiian Macaroni Salad, 77
    Kale Mashed Potatoes, 138–139
    Loco Moco Nachos, 36
    Perfect Pork Loin with Chunky
        Applesauce, 146–147
    Simply Fantastic Gravy, 138–139
    Spicy Veggie Lasagna, 58–59
    Tantalizing Texas-Style Bean Soup, 125
    Tasty Turkey Picadillo Cups, 103
onions, green
    Fluffy Green Onion Cloud Eggs, 15
    Grilled Turkey-Apple Burgers, 83
    Hawaiian Macaroni Salad, 77
    Mac and Cheese Station, 35
    Mini Sausage Corn Pups, 29
    Mouthwatering Chicken
        Mole Tostadas, 121
    Spicy Creamy Cheesy Corn, 143
    Tiny Thai Basil Beef Bowls, 105
    Zestylicious Mexi Layered Dip, 32
onions, red
    Blackened Flank Steak
        and Corny Salsa, 61
    Mulli Guacamole, 33
    Pimento Dip, 71
    Zestylicious Mexi Layered Dip, 32
Ooey Gooey Hot Curry Cambozola Dip, 5
orange juice
    Orange Shandys, 69
    Sublime Sangria (Boozy
        and Not Boozy), 91
oranges
    Mandarin Cream Delights, 131
    Orange Shandys, 69
    Sublime Sangria (Boozy
        and Not Boozy), 91

P

Parmesan cheese
    Almondy Caesar Salad, 53
    Antipasto Salad, 75
    Baked Bacon Crackers, 31
    Breakfast-y Pasta Salad, 11

Cheesy Egg and Polenta Casserole, 13
French Onion Soup Stuffed
   Mushrooms, 137
Kale Mashed Potatoes, 138–139
Lemony Fettucine Alfredo, 57
Mac and Cheese Station, 35
Mulli Guacamole, 33
Primo Parmesan-Crusted
   Chicken Strips, 127

parsley
   Grilled Turkey-Apple Burgers, 83

Partridges in Pear Trees, 3

Party Popovers, 51

pasta
   Breakfast-y Pasta Salad, 11
   Hawaiian Macaroni Salad, 77
   Lemony Fettucine Alfredo, 57
   Mac and Cheese Station, 35
   Spicy Veggie Lasagna, 58–59

peaches
   Pretzel Salad Cups, 87
   Sublime Sangria (Boozy
     and Not Boozy), 91

peanut butter
   Mouthwatering Chicken
     Mole Tostadas, 121

pear juice
   Partridges in Pear Trees, 3

pears
   Alluring Arugula Pear Salad, 119
   Antipasto Salad, 75
   Sublime Sangria (Boozy
     and Not Boozy), 91

peas
   Breakfast-y Pasta Salad, 11

pecans
   Alluring Arugula Pear Salad, 119
   Antipasto Salad, 75
   Aunt Pat's Chocolate Espresso
     Cream "Pie," 153
   Chocolaty Goodness Coffee Cake, 19

Ooey Gooey Hot Curry
   Cambozola Dip, 5
Perfect Pork Loin with Chunky
   Applesauce, 146–147

pepper jack cheese
   Pimento Dip, 71

peppers, bell
   Mouthwatering Chicken
     Mole Tostadas, 121
   Spicy Veggie Lasagna, 58–59
   Tasty Turkey Picadillo Cups, 103
   Tiny Thai Basil Beef Bowls, 105

Perfect Pork Loin with Chunky
   Applesauce, 146–147

pickles
   Cubano Tots! 49
   Pickle-Craving Finger Sandwiches, 101

pico de gallo salsa
   The Quick(est) and Easy(iest)
     Amazing Layered Dip, 115

pie crust
   Princess Leia Cinnamon
     Roll Apple Pie, 21

Pilsner beer
   Beer-Perol Surprises, 25

Pimento Dip, 71

Pimm's #1
   Pimm's Cups, 113
   Spicy Holiday Lemonade, 134–135

pineapple, crushed
   Hawaiian Slaw, 37
   Hazelnutty Goodness
     Carrot Cupcakes, 129
   Pretzel Salad Cups, 87

Pineapple Bacon Upside-Down Cake, 63

pineapple marmalade
   Lovely and Lemony Olive Oil Cake, 107

pinto beans
   Tantalizing Texas-Style Bean Soup, 125

Pistachio Cake Cups, Chocolate
   Cold Brew, 85

Pita Walking Taco Snack Bags, Greek, 117
Polenta Casserole, Cheesy Egg and, 13
Popovers, Party, 51
Pork Loin with Chunky Applesauce, Perfect, 146–147
potato chips
    Can't-Eat-Just-One Western Sliders, 122
    Honey-Butter Shortbread Cookies, 43
potatoes
    Chorizo Hash, 17
    Kale Mashed Potatoes, 138–139
Pretzel Salad Cups, 87
Primo Parmesan-Crusted Chicken Strips, 127
Princess Leia Cinnamon Roll Apple Pie, 21
prosecco
    Lemon Chiffon Punch, 47
    Partridges in Pear Trees, 3
    Strawberry Bubblies, 113
provolone cheese
    Loco Moco Nachos, 36
pudding mix, chocolate
    Aunt Pat's Chocolate Espresso Cream "Pie," 153
pudding mix, vanilla
    Mandarin Cream Delights, 131
Puttanesca Sauce, 58

Q

Quick(est) and Easy(iest) Amazing Layered Dip, The, 115

R

radishes
    Zestylicious Mexi Layered Dip, 32
raisins
    Tasty Turkey Picadillo Cups, 103
raspberries
    Watermelon-Mint Salad, 73
refried beans
    Zestylicious Mexi Layered Dip, 32
rice
    Loco Moco Nachos, 36
    Tantalizing Texas-Style Bean Soup, 125
    Tiny Thai Basil Beef Bowls, 105
    Your New Favorite Coconut-Cilantro Rice, 97
ricotta cheese
    Spicy Veggie Lasagna, 58–59
Roasted Vegetables, 58
romaine
    Grilled Chicken Cobb Salad, 81
rosé, sparkling
    Fizzy Fun Pink Lemonade, 3
    Strawberry Bubblies, 113
Rosemary Spiced Candied Bacon, 7
Roxanne, 23
rum
    Hemingway Daiquiris, 69
    Tom and Jerrys, 134

S

salads
    Alluring Arugula Pear Salad, 119
    Almondy Caesar Salad, 53
    Antipasto Salad, 75
    Delectable Curry Chicken Salad, 95
    Grilled Chicken Cobb Salad, 81
    Hawaiian Macaroni Salad, 77
    Tim's Turkey Milanese with Arugula Salad, 144–145
    Watermelon-Mint Salad, 73
salami
    Antipasto Salad, 75
saltine crackers
    Cocktail Meatballs with Grape Jelly, 27
    Lemon-Lime Chiffon Pie, Oh My! 109
Sangria (Boozy and Not Boozy), Sublime, 91

sausage
    Cheesy Egg and Polenta Casserole, 13
    Chorizo Hash, 17
    Mini Sausage Corn Pups, 29
    The Quick(est) and Easy(iest)
        Amazing Layered Dip, 115

7-up
    Spicy Holiday Lemonade, 134–135

shallots
    Can't-Eat-Just-One
        Western Sliders, 122
    Lemony Fettucine Alfredo, 57
    Mac and Cheese Station, 35

Shortbread Cookies, Honey-Butter, 43

sides
    BBQ Beans with Turkey Bacon, 79
    Blueberry Almond Butter Smoothies, 9
    Breakfast-y Pasta Salad, 11
    Cup o' Grapes Fruit Salad, 99
    Fried Brussels with Appley-
        Fenneley Slaw, 141
    Spicy Creamy Cheesy Corn, 143
    Your New Favorite Coconut-
        Cilantro Rice, 97
    Yummus! Yogurt Dip, 55

Simply Fantastic Gravy, 138–139
Soup, Tantalizing Texas-Style Bean, 125

sour cream
    Chocolaty Goodness Coffee Cake, 19
    Lovely and Lemony Olive Oil Cake, 107
    Mandarin Cream Delights, 131
    Mini-Chicken and Waffles, 39
    The Quick(est) and Easy(iest)
        Amazing Layered Dip, 115
    Zestylicious Mexi Layered Dip, 32

soy sauce
    Mouthwatering Chicken
        Mole Tostadas, 121
    Tiny Thai Basil Beef Bowls, 105

Soyrizo
    The Quick(est) and Easy(iest)
        Amazing Layered Dip, 115

Spicy Creamy Cheesy Corn, 143
Spicy Holiday Lemonade, 134–135
Spicy Veggie Lasagna, 58–59

spinach
    Antipasto Salad, 75
    Cheesy Egg and Polenta Casserole, 13

Spoons, 45

strawberries
    Pimm's Cups, 113
    Strawberry Bubblies, 113
    Sublime Sangria (Boozy
        and Not Boozy), 91

sweetened condensed milk
    Lemon-Lime Chiffon Pie, Oh My! 109
    No-Churn Ice Cream, 150–151

Swiss cheese
    Cubano Tots! 49

T

Taleggio cheese
    Spicy Creamy Cheesy Corn, 143
    Taleggio Cheese Sauce, 127

Tantalizing Texas-Style Bean Soup, 125
Tasty Turkey Picadillo Cups, 103

Tater Tots
    Cubano Tots! 49

Thumper, 23
Tim's Turkey Milanese with
    Arugula Salad, 144–145
Tiny Thai Basil Beef Bowls, 105
Tom and Jerrys, 134

tomato sauce
    Tasty Turkey Picadillo Cups, 103

tomatoes
    Antipasto Salad, 75
    Blackened Flank Steak
        and Corny Salsa, 61
    Greek Pita Walking Taco Snack Bags, 117

Grilled Chicken Cobb Salad, 81
Mouthwatering Chicken
   Mole Tostadas, 121
Spicy Veggie Lasagna, 58–59
Tantalizing Texas-Style Bean Soup, 125
tortillas
   Loco Moco Nachos, 36
Tostadas, Mouthwatering
   Chicken Mole, 121
turkey, ground
   Greek Pita Walking Taco Snack Bags, 117
   Grilled Turkey-Apple Burgers, 83
   Tasty Turkey Picadillo Cups, 103
turkey breasts
   Tim's Turkey Milanese with
     Arugula Salad, 144–145

V

vodka
   Spicy Holiday Lemonade, 134–135
   Vodka Giddyups, 25

W

Waffles, Mini-Chicken and, 39
walnuts
   Antipasto Salad, 75
water chestnuts
   Cocktail Meatballs with Grape Jelly, 27
Watermelon-Mint Salad, 73
wheat beer
   Orange Shandys, 69
whipped cream/topping
   Aunt Pat's Chocolate Espresso
     Cream "Pie," 153
   Chocolate Cold Brew Pistachio
     Cake Cups, 85
   Lemon-Lime Chiffon Pie, Oh My! 109
   Mandarin Cream Delights, 131
   Pretzel Salad Cups, 87
wine, red
   French Onion Soup Stuffed
     Mushrooms, 137
wine, rosé
   Sublime Sangria (Boozy
     and Not Boozy), 91
wine, white
   Lemon Chiffon Punch, 47

Y

yogurt
   Blueberry Almond Butter Smoothies, 9
   Cup o' Grapes Fruit Salad, 99
   Greek Pita Walking Taco Snack Bags, 117
   Lovely and Lemony Olive Oil Cake, 107
   Yummus! Yogurt Dip, 55
Your New Favorite Coconut-Cilantro Rice
   Loco Moco Nachos, 36
   recipe, 97
   Tiny Thai Basil Beef Bowls, 105
Yummus! Yogurt Dip, 55

Z

Zestylicious Mexi Layered Dip, 32

www.ingramcontent.com/pod-product-compliance
Lightning Source LLC
Chambersburg PA
CBHW041137170426

43198CB00023B/2978